Isle of Flowers

Isle of Flowers

Poems by Florida's Individual Artist Fellows

Introduction by
Judith Kitchen

Edited by Donna J. Long,
Helen Pruitt Wallace,
and Rick Campbell

Anhinga Press   *Tallahassee, Florida*

© Copyright Anhinga Press, 1995

No portion of this book may be reproduced in any form without the written permission of the publisher, except by a reviewer who may quote brief passages in connection with a review for a newspaper or magazine.

Publication of this book was made possible by grants from the Florida Department of State, Division of Cultural Affairs, and the Florida Arts Council. Anhinga Press also wishes to thank the staff of the Florida Department of State, Division of Cultural Affairs, for research assistance on this project.

Cover Art: "Pier in Twilight" by Dean Gioia
Cover Design by Lynne Knight
Book Design and Production by Toni L. Whitfield
    and John E. Simpson

Library of Congress Cataloging-in-Publication Data:

Isle of Flowers: Poems by Florida's Individual Artist Fellows / edited by Donna J. Long, Helen Pruitt Wallace, and Rick Campbell, and with an introduction by Judith Kitchen. — 1st ed.

ISBN 0-938078-39-9
ISBN 0-938078-41-0 (pbk.)
Library of Congress Cataloging Card Number 95-078814

Anhinga Press Inc. is a nonprofit corporation dedicated wholly to the publication and appreciation of fine poetry. For personal orders, catalogues, and information, write to: Anhinga Press, P.O. Box 10595, Tallahassee FL 32302

Printed in the United States of America
First Edition, 1995

Poets appear in *Isle of Flowers* chronologically by year of their earliest Florida Individual Artist Fellowship, and, when more than one poet received fellowships in the same year, alphabetically by the poets' last names. Exceptions to this order were made only in cases where adhering to it would have compromised the visual integrity of two-page poems.

All text in *Isle of Flowers* is set in a Garamond face provided by Elfring Soft Fonts. Unlike many latter-day Garamonds, which are based on the so-called *Typi Academiae* cut around 1615 by Jean Jannon, Elfring's Garamond derives from the original designs by Claude Garamond; these designs first appeared in books printed in Paris around 1532—twenty years after Ponce de Leon's voyage to the real Isle of Flowers.

Message from the Florida Secretary of State

The Florida Division of Cultural Affairs, Department of State's Florida Individual Artist Fellowship program was established in 1976 and is designed to recognize practicing professional artists residing in the state through monetary fellowship awards. The program provides support for artists of exceptional talent and demonstrated ability to improve their artistic skills and enhance their careers. Fellowships are offered in eight disciplines: dance; folk arts; interdisciplinary; media arts; music; theatre; visual arts and crafts; and of particular relevance to this poetry anthology, literature.

Over the years, hundreds of fellowships have been awarded. Of these, thirty-four poets are represented in *Isle of Flowers*, the first literary anthology of fellowship recipients ever published. Many of these fellowship recipients have gone on to attain national acclaim in the literary world. Anhinga Press is also gaining stature and recognition on a national level due to its publication of books of the highest literary merit and distinct regional flavor. Just as Anhinga Press frequently provides emerging poets with their first major career stepping stone, the Division's fellowships often serve that same purpose at the state level.

Florida is home to a vibrant and rapidly growing cultural community and is gaining a national recognition as a cultural leader. Florida ranks third nationally in state Legislative appropriations to culture and the arts.

Individual artists contribute enormously to Florida's arts community. According to the 1990 U.S. Census, Florida now ranks fourth nationally in individual artist population. A significant portion of these artists are writers.

As Chief Cultural Officer of Florida, I congratulate the initiative and determination of Anhinga Press to make this anthology a reality. *Isle of Flowers* establishes a public and historical record of nearly twenty years' worth of Florida Individual Artist Fellowship poetry recipients. I am confident that this anthology of exceptional quality will enhance the stature of both the poets participating and Anhinga Press itself.

Sandra B. Mortham
Secretary of State

Table of Contents

Introduction by Judith Kitchen   v

Van K. Brock   1
The Hindenberg ♦ This is not a love poem ♦ Sunday Morning with Prokofiev ♦ Cold Front ♦ Epistle for the Cicadas

Jeffrey Knapp   10
A Line of Turkey Buzzards Surveys I-95 ♦ Fernando : Life : Time

Peter Meinke   12
Azaleas ♦ Scars ♦ The Perch ♦ The Attack ♦ Liquid Paper

Stephen Corey   19
Learning to Live in America ♦ Belief ♦ Failure To Be Priests: A Modern Harvest ♦ Taking the Light Whitely ♦ Migration ♦ Deaf and Mute

Lola Haskins   26
A Confluence ♦ Matanzas ♦ How I Learned ♦ Uchepas ♦ The Prodigy

G.S. Sharat Chandra   31
Immigrants of Loss ♦ At the Burning-Ghats ♦ Love Rites ♦ Identities

Joanne Childers   37
Tracking Halley's Comet ♦ Garden-Touring with Aunt Mae ♦ This Reminder

Brandon Kershner   41
Tantrum ♦ Scotoma ♦ Responsibilities ♦ What It Is ♦ Dredging

P.V. LeForge — 47
 Sweater ♦ Anting ♦ Those Moments That Make Us Remember We're Alive ♦ The Secret Life of Moles

W.C. Morton — 54
 River Rats ♦ Intimations ♦ In a Tree Stand West of Raleigh ♦ Florida Prelude

Edmund Skellings — 58
 Incantation ♦ Heartwood ♦ The Leningrad Writers Conference 1942

Eugenie Nable — 63
 The Elephant Mother and Her Baby at the Tampa Carnival ♦ The Fish Man ♦ A Late Night Telegram to Dr. Christiaan Barnard

Nancy Powell Rousseau — 71
 J. Ford in the Water Hyacinths ♦ Cherry Hammock ♦ Seminole Indian Jacket ♦ They Write From Great Distances

Sam Harrison — 77
 A Poem about ~~Substance~~ Sustenance Spaniels ♦ The Last Great Invention ♦ Air Waves ♦ A Laundromat in Mt. Kisco

Yvonne Sapia — 83
 Fertile Crescent ♦ The Exile Tree ♦ Parts of the Verb "To Be"

Hal Shows — 90
 Camellias ♦ Sonnet ♦ Ode on a Train

Laurence Donovan — 94
 Dog Island IV ♦ Dog Island IX ♦ The Traveler

Donald Justice — 98
 A Winter Ode to the Old Men of Lummus Park, Miami, Florida ♦ Variations on a Text by Vallejo

David Kirby   *100*
    *The King Is Dead ♦ Complicity ♦ I Think I Am Going to
Call My Wife Paraguay ♦ Baths*

A. McA. Miller   *109*
    Rowing ♦ Her Olds "Firenza" ♦ Obsession

Enid Shomer   *115*
    *Global Aphasia ♦ Sun and Moon in Mrs. Sussman's Tap
Dancing Class ♦ Cadillac ♦ Elegy And Rant For My Father
♦ Floating Islands*

Rick Campbell   *123*
    *Hard Love ♦ Hanging Tobacco ♦ Leaving Home, Pittsburgh,
1966 ♦ Ohio River Sunday ♦ The Geography of Desire*

Christy Sheffield Sanford   *129*
    *Traveling through Ports that Begin with "M" ♦
Hurricane! Alex!*

Barbara Hamby   *134*
    *The Language of Bees ♦ St. Anthony of the Floating Larynx
♦ The Ovary Tattoo*

Judith Berke   *140*
    *Poem Beginning in the Bed of My Mother and Father ♦
The Strangler Fig ♦ Madre Del Olvido ♦ Triple Toe Loop ♦
We Know Now*

Silvia Curbelo   *146*
    *Photograph of My Parents ♦ Drinking Song ♦ Tonight I
Can Almost Hear the Singing ♦ Last Call ♦ Bedtime Stories
♦ The Lake Has Swallowed the Whole Sky*

Steve Kronen   *156*
    *The World Before Them ♦ In the Hangar of Brisbee,
Oklahoma, 1933 ♦ The Awful Balance ♦ Mayflies*

Gail Shepherd   *162*
    The Owl ♦ First Questions ♦ Girls at Confirmation ♦
    Southern Weddings

Peter Hargitai   *168*
    Cats ♦ The Art of Taxidermy ♦ Seeds ♦ Mother's Visit No. 29

Alison Kolodinsky   *173*
    march ♦ In Carroll County, New Hampshire ♦ Absence ♦
    Inventing the Wind

Peter Schmitt   *179*
    Glance ♦ A Day at the Beach ♦ Under Desks ♦ Homecoming
    ♦ Tin Ear

Susan Mitchell   *186*
    From the Journals of the Frog Prince ♦ Havana Birth ♦
    The Kiss

Hunt Hawkins   *192*
    Skating ♦ Honeymoon ♦ The Prejohn ♦ Apnea ♦ Pennies

Stephen Gibson   *200*
    American Primitive ♦ The Bacchae: The Deaths of Benito
    Mussolini and Claretta Petacci, Milan, April 29, 1945 ♦
    The Bra ♦ The Answer

Sharon Weightman   *204*
    My Children Know Reggae ♦ A Prayer for My Quadroon
    Daughter ♦ On Monroe Street ♦ Night Song ♦ In Time

Biographical Notes   *210*

Acknowledgments   *218*

Introduction

March 1st, upstate New York. There's snow on the ground and the occasional fat flake in the air, although the sun is shining. Our weather man reports that March has come in "like a lamb with an attitude." So it's a good time to be reading poems from Florida, poets who have, over the years, been selected for a grant from the Florida Arts Council. March, Peter Meinke's "Azaleas" reminds me, is when the "white azaleas open to the air," bursting forth from the flares they appeared to be in December. And Miami, Donald Justice reminds me, is where old men have been "blown south" to sit on benches, where Justice himself (in "Variations on a Text by Vallejo") wishes to die on a Sunday, in the sun, the buildings white in its glare and the grave diggers resting a moment in the shade of the palms.

There is something exotic here to the northern eye. The imagery is not only of the palm trees and azaleas, but of the cypresses and ceiling fans in Alison Kolodinsky's "Inventing the Wind" or the "wrist-thick" moccasins and unhurried Suwannee in Lola Haskins' "A Confluence" or the curving lights along the bay in Silvia Curbelo's "Tonight I Can Almost Hear the Singing." In Enid Shomer's sea it's warm enough to float for an hour like "two shy camellias," and Peter Schmitt's geese return to the lake at the end, not the beginning, of the summer.

There is also something exotic to the ear. Music is everywhere—from Prokofiev and Mozart to Elvis, Leadbelly, and Tyrone Davis. It surfaces in the dressmaker's songs and in the humming afternoons of a tropical climate. It surfaces also in Stephen Corey's lush sonnet paying linguistic homage to Hopkins and the repeated patterns (like cut glass) in Rick Campbell's villanelle.

The poems in *Isle of Flowers*, to borrow a phrase from Campbell's "The Geography of Desire," seem to be "living on the border." Silvia Curbelo's poems carry the undercurrent of the Spanish language and this is echoed in the music (and syntax) of Susan Mitchell's "Havana Birth." The poems in this collection also explore the Eastern European background of Peter Hargitai, the Jewish roots of Enid Shomer, and the Oklahoma childhood of Steve Kronen.

Along with diversity of cultural backgrounds, the poets in this volume exhibit a diversity of styles: the long, conversational lines of Barbara Hamby or of David Kirby, who has found an innovative way to advance the art of storytelling; the long, formal lines of Stephen Gibson or Enid Shomer, whose slant rhymes tease the ear; the short, fluid lines and dazzling leaps of Lola Haskins; the short, staccato lines of Brandon Kershner; the formal tension of Judith Berke and measured cadences of Donald Justice. They also have diversity of tone, ranging from the political (Van K. Brock and Stephen Gibson) to the contemplative (Steve Kronen and Stephen Corey) to the humorous (Peter Meinke) to the more than humorous (Hunt Hawkins' "The Prejohn"—a poem whose reputation preceded it north—which turns a cold eye on our culture by observing "the little room you enter / before you get to the bathroom").

This is a valuable anthology. It not only reacquaints me with the work of poets I have admired for years but introduces me to the work of others with whom I was not so familiar. I am pleased to discover Enid Shomer's marvelous vowel music, Susan Mitchell's startling similes, and David Kirby's hilarious roundabout forays into his own mind. More than that, the careful selection of these poems underscores the way a collection can come to mean more than the sum of its parts.

Reading these poems, I am struck, not so much by their physical geography as by their emotional terrain. The objects of desire are many. Passionate, profound, and provocative, the imaginations here inhabit the interior and exterior, honkytonk and dancehall and skating rink, the collective summer vacations of the past (fish and fishing run through this collection), and the landscape of dream and memory. The desire here is not so much for place as for connection, and connection is illusory at best. It's more than Curbelo's "pure want" or Mitchell's "muteness / about to blossom." Stephen Corey sees it "illumined / by that which must touch without touching." Judith Berke names it "the absolute / separateness / at the very moment / we disappear into each other."

In the end, the inchoate assumes the contours of the physical. "The world belongs to the world," says Silvia Curbelo. In *Isle of Flowers*, the world is given back to us, transformed again and again by the poets' shaping visions. "This is not a love poem," Van Brock insists—all the while loving the land and its lost past. "Sometimes we love almost enough," Curbelo answers. "I would have saved them..." begins Brandon Kershner's wry twist on human responsibility. But only with "endless vigilance" suggests Peter Schmitt. And all the while Judith Berke's skater is poised in the middle of a triple toe loop, flying "against the earth, and in love with it." Shore birds peck the sand, freighters steer for the islands, and the surf drums and drums its monotone at the edges of the land, wedding past with present, there with here.

Isle of Flowers reminds us that poetry knows no borders, that experience is universal, and that Florida sunshine is an especially important catalyst for poetry. I look out my window. Darkness, a few shimmery flakes in the streetlight—a northern version of those thin petals falling on the walk, an "ideal of vulnerability made palpable."

Judith Kitchen
Brockport, NY

And believing that this land was an island, they named it *La Florida*, because it has a very beautiful view of many cool woodlands, and it was level and uniform; and because, moreover, they discovered it in the time of the *Feast of Flowers*.

Antonio de Herrera

Van K. Brock

The Hindenberg

This early showpiece of the Thousand Year Reich used 850,000 skins of cattle for hydrogen bags.

It is said that the night it burned
the thunder of panicking hooves
drowned the screams of passengers.

As far away as the buttes of Asia,
one old Siberian woman says that merely
the echo of their lowing still stirs
immense winds and whirlwinds.
                              All the small
meadows of Europe remember their grazing,
cattle-cars and railway platforms shudder
still at their foreshadowings.
                              Untold cobblers
recall the million seams glued and stitched
on screaming machines before their pockets
held enough hydrogen to kindle a conflagration.

The war on nature begun,
eventually, every country in Europe
and many in Africa and Asia were gutted:
in bombings, in battle, at sea, and in the fires,
filth, and hunger of virulent slave pens:
the outward rendering of ageless accumulations
sucked up from the cities and villages of earth,
and the ruins run in and out of us all,
stretching before and behind
for far more than a Thousand Years.

This is not a love poem

It is a tracker looking for the last milligram
of serotonin in exhausted blood,
looking for holes in the history of hunger
with its fragrance of hewn sandalwood.

This is not a love song. Listen.
It is the wind on a prairie where
there are no buffalo and no smoke rises
in the long winter without villages;

this is the muffled sound in the iron rails
spiked to the hewn bodies of the lost forests
of the cry and smoke of the loco horse
full of people who are not my people—

soldiers, horses, and men hungry for land
women hungry to breed with land
that is not my land or theirs or anyone's,
as I am no one's and no one is mine.

You hear the sound of the owl and coyote
where the land has been ravaged of wolves,
the sound of your heart recalling the rapid beat
beat of the tom-tom calling him home,

the man who never returned, whose horse
never returned with the quiver you made
from the skin of badger he pierced
with his quivering arrow, the woman

you wanted to be and thought you had lost
until the tracker found you under mounds of grief
where the long search through many men
left a trail that wound through the future.

Here the fragrance of flowers too sweet
and too short lived, the musk of dried skins
grown brittle, the scent of the long grass,
reaching and reaching in every direction,

finds only the wind the prairie bows
before, the lost sound of wild rivers dammed
and tamed: there will be no more love poems,
only this dream from which no one awakes.

Sunday Morning with Prokofiev

Nicole pulls open my shirt to beep my nipple.
I beep hers. We've more in common than a house.
She brings her wrapped doll, moors it
on my chest, and goes away. Her father
lives 500 miles from here, nor am I her lover,
husband, or even grandfather. Mushroomed
on this red beanbag like a giant elf
in a stretching world among Prokofiev's
hammered, pedalled, bowed, plucked strings,
I am a scraped surface on which to write.

What she writes on me is herself.
Too much alive at two to lie so still,
she wanders through the house, testing
world after world, while I, seven times seven,
grandma's consort, though having many worlds
still to explore, have distilled patience,
once lacked, from time, that she may redeem
this morning for herself, me, this red beanbag,
her doll, and Prokofiev.

Whatever can free her or any of us,
a fierce force tells her to leave her child
on the grizzly, heaving delta of my chest,
as Miriam left Moses for fathering reeds
to stroke on mother Nile. My marshes
all underground, my hard breast rises
and falls as tides of blood and air stretch
and contract the hollow my missing rib
left shrunken with absence.

My son, emerging from his clef of pure Rock
into this spacious universe of Prokofiev
where I float, half-Moses, half-Odysseus,
asks a Cyclopean question, voice deep into
its second decade, "Why's a grown man holding

a doll?" I might have said with Odysseus,
"I am Noman," a wanderer in a wilderness,
but I say, "I am holding it for Nicole."
Child, woman, it's you I rock on the hard hill
of my chest where the caved winds keep time

with the music—for him, his brother, me, you—
it's your mother, your aunts, your grandmother
and every woman I ever loved from afar—so much
and so well that the well swallows the rope.
Yet my fingers pat and caress, that the man
who grows in you and the woman great in me,
with child too large to contain, can love,
understand, or free for themselves and each other.

Cold Front

The blue Virginia sky is cast with uniform gray.
Trees, some with names I don't know, ridge
distant purple mountains where mist rises,
and publish a continuum in every value of green
they patiently revise with gold and red.
A few have already withered and browned.
New England, New York, New Jersey are under snow,
entire landscapes whited out. We feel it here,
filtering the sun. Climates everywhere
sense it. Miami sizzles, freezes.

Only last week a blue heron flew back and forth above
as I crawled in the lake, neither of us understanding,
as I swam on my back looking up, then face down
into a pale suspension of earth and water
and saw a woman, looking back, eyes like mine,
lipless mouth forming words, hair flowing.
If this was what the heron saw, flying above me,
our nets found only iron weights tied to a plastic
milkjug full of concrete, dragging a frayed rope.

We have put on jeans and jackets over our shorts
and the grazing cattle cluster closer to the old
tongueless wagons that serve as winter mangers.
New growths will burst from a snow-splotched earth
where small insects live seconds, while others
become locusts, moths, totally new forms, whirring
over arrowheads, whistling. Schools are out today,
and the evening news ends with its usual frosting:
laughing children among snowmen on Capital Hill,
only two hours away, shape iceballs and slide down
the slopes. The president is laughing, waving.

The Holsteins turn into black and white abstractions.
A wind breathes in the trees, and they have begun
to stipple our lawn with walnuts and colored leaves.

Edging the pasture, tall goldenrod go on shouting
dominant yellow blossoms at Algonquian bloodweeds,
whose deep red leaves and pokeberries, turning
into wine, rise in quiet explosions among them.

                    1987

Epistle for the Cicadas

Did I not, from larva, grow a shell, then crawl
from it, skinless, leaving my theologies
and causes clasped to trees—so why have my maps
and chronicles brought me again to this green lathe?
My eyes still turn from blue to green
with what I wear, moving like giddy parakeets
from sky to trees. But your brown eyes are pools
in mountain streams that flash with quartz, amber
and speckled trout. If I seem to walk on water,
I step from stone to stone, barely beneath the surface
on slippery maps of mystery, still awkwardly holding
the old buts, ands, and thoughs. Yet coasting
out of the Rockies, without brakes, I loved
the muffled psalms of tires on well-banked curves
as I clutched and geared toward valleys,
out of snowfall, past bursts of red
on the thawing shoulders, to discover
the relation of rain to crocuses, the heat blast,
the seared leaves: terrible simplicities.

After twenty years together, we know so much
of each other and so little. When I break
inside, like a twig, my fingers flower.
The cicada has uttered itself out of its shell
and flown away on the woven transparencies
of our longings scattering its three songs—
of friendship, love, danger. We have heard the wind
inquiring vainly through its small, translucent igloo
in other houses in Cedar Rapids, Kew, Atlanta,
Corrib, Aretina, Amelia, Via di Mezzo.

The thin syntax of glazed shell flattens;
a rough echo of syllables scans the rubble;
from opposite ends of a long row of carrels,
we pass, eyes wrestling, and are brought back
to where I first saw you, not entirely lost

in reading—our knowledge, desire, reverie
twisting a rope of their own—your hair
already indelibly imprinted on a page
in the long reading room where you slept.
Was it where she sits or he, half in, half out
of his story that I dreamed Alexandria when
the assembled lore of the ages burst into flames?
And from the tinder crackled whole civilizations,
as they gushed and exploded their distilled
loves long and plain over the fiery petals.
The deeper the springs the calmer they seem,
and no one can know without diving, how far
and breathless his reflection goes. By the time
we discover who we are, every cell inside
has died and been reborn, and again.
We often see the empty shells on the bark,
seldom the cicadas alight amidst green needles
and leaves, or whirring over us, their wings
whispering our gospels and histories,
the endless song of our revelations,
translating us again into transparent tongues.

Jeffrey Knapp

A Line of Turkey Buzzards Surveys I-95

On the 45th anniversary of the bombing of Pearl Harbor

A line of turkey buzzards surveys I-95
But the only carrion it finds are the dead brain cells of memory

I didn't know in 1961 that when Caro's Florist closed on Friday
And reopened Monday as a fallout shelter store it was a metaphor

That memory on the 45th anniversary of the bombing of Pearl
Harbor seems as old as DNA

The lick of night puts memory to sleep for all but the largest
Buzzards, the ones who drive Mercedes under their own wings

Hitler drove a Mercedes, that's for sure,
Remember?

Memory sticks to you like scales to a fish
But the fishmonger's knife is sharp

And near

Fernando : Life : Time

for Fernando Garcia, who died of AIDS

My daughter likes to say
That if our cat were a person
She'd be 95 years old!

If you were a cat,
Fernando,
You'd be 250

And if a lemur, 350
And if a platypus, 500
Or a bat, 2,475

But if you were a ray of light,
Fernando,
You'd be 264,410,536,100,000,000 miles

With galaxies between us just the same

Peter Meinke

Azaleas

In the morning, in December
they lean like flares over our brick pathway,
vessels of fragrant energy,
their bright explosions enclosed by the frailest membrane:
they tremble with their holy repressions.
We watch; we tremble, too. We learn.

They thrive on acid, these azaleas; they burn
in darkness, loving the shadows of old oaks
whose broken leaves flutter down to feed
their flowering fantasies.

For surely azaleas are not real, they grow
in some deep wilderness of soul, some known
ideal of vulnerability made palpable,
whose thin petals float dying to the ground
even as we walk by, without touching.
Our very presence seems to kill.

We know more than we can say: we live
in waves of feeling and awareness
where images unfold and grow
along the leafwork of our nerves and veins;
and when one morning late in March
we walk out on our porch and see
the white azaleas open to the air
we recognize them from our dreams
as every cell projects our affirmation.

O Pride of Mobile, Maiden Blush,
Prince of Orange, President Clay:

the names are humorous examples
of human hubris—O Glory of Sunninghill!
And yet they're touching, too: my salmon-
colored Duc de Rohan's fragile aristocracy
doomed like his forebears to lose his head;
your Elegans, that early bloomer,
whose petals lie like butterflies on our walk
or pastel Kleenex thickly strewn
in some orgy of melancholy weeping....

Dwarves and Giants, Pinkshell, Flame—
O my dear, so many azaleas are dying!
We must have a party! Here! This afternoon!

Scars

When I was young   I longed for scars
like my father's   They were the best
scars on the block   startling   varied
pink as a tongue against his whiskey skin

The longest bolted from his elbow
finger-thick where the barbed wire plunged in
a satin rip thinning toward the wrist
I read the riddle of my father's body

like a legend punctuated by pale hyphens
neat commas   surgical asterisks and exclamation
points from scalp to ankle   His tragic knuckles
spoke violence in demotic Greek

My silent father said little   too little   it seems
but after the divorce he told me   tracing
the curved path on his skull where hair never grew
'It's the ones you can't see that kill you'

and it's true our doctor said his liver
which did him in   was scarred like an old war horse
Still   the mark I knew best I gave him myself   hitting
a pop fly straight up and swinging the child's bat again

with all my might as the ball descended
over the plate   He had run in to catch it
and the bat cracked him under his chin   dropping
my father like a murdered king   peeling a wound

no butterfly bandage could cover   I was too stunned
to move   but the look my mother gave me proved
no matter what happened later   this man bleeding
like Laius on the ground was the one she loved

The Perch

That day in the canoe
the summer sun poured down
like angel butter and I sat
for hours without a nibble,
the lake flat as a fry pan.
Only the limp, torn cardboard
of last night's celebrations
disturbed the surface until
my bobber lurched, the pole
humped, and I pulled
a yellow perch into the fifth of July.

Plump as a pillow—
but too little and too late
to make a meal for us—
he'd swallowed the bait
and his scarlet gills gaped
like knife wounds
as I twisted the crooked hook
to yank it out, his barred
bloodshot breast snapping,
and I cut my hand on his fins
before dropping him in the lake.

It was still ninety degrees
at the dock when I shouldered
the canoe, staggering up our steep
steps—and suddenly my breath
blew from my lungs, the Adirondacks swirled
around me, a red wire circled
my chest and flung me to the ground,
the canoe pinning my leg like a worm
near the rack. Someone
held me over the edge of something—
and threw me back.

The Attack

Huffing by the butcher I see my heart
impaled on a hook   bloody hunk of fat
venial and menial as a bureaucrat
stumping for reelection   It's an art
this hanging in there past one's prime
until it can't remember why it beats
but just repeats   repeats   repeats
like an idiot confessing to a crime

I dream I clean it   peel it   scrub
it to the grain...   For years I burned
to be pure hard oak   but somehow turned
this shapeless lump   this tired turnip
humped in rain   rooted in mud   Yesterday
at the Gallery I leaned over to see
Pissarro's *La Côte des Boeufs*   and something
tore loose inside   I dropped as if to pray

on the dusty floor   alarming the passersby
and guard who sat me down
to give me water with reproachful frown:
bad form to die
among the Impressionists
whose flickering canvases urge
us to live more boldly   a surge
of sunlight bolting from their wrists

like lightning from God's finger   "Hypo-
glycemia" I told the guard   "I'll be quite
all right..."   He repeated "Quite"
but wouldn't let me go
until I swore I wouldn't sue the place
and at last limped out into the winter sun
where a cripple shook his tin of coins
like a dirty fist below my dirty face

The signs for all diseases are the same:
nausea   a racing heart   cold
sweat: it's boring   the old
story   except when it's *your* name
on the toe tag   And even then
from a philosophical
point of view it's laughable...
so I turn back and enter

the shop   All that meat   hanging
there   couldn't be more
politically incorrect   My poor
heart whanging
like a shotgun   well what the hell:
I look fondly at the ribs   the flanks
the patties   kidneys   glands
chops   brains   And bang the bell

Liquid Paper

Smooth as a snail, this little parson
pardons our sins. Touch the brush tip
lightly and—*abracadabra!*—a clean slate.

We know those who blot their brains
by sniffing it, which shows
it erases more than ink
and with imagination anything
can be misapplied.... In the army,
our topsergeant drank aftershave, squeezing
my Old Spice to the last slow drop.

It worked like Liquid Paper in his head

until he'd glide across the streets of Heidelberg
hunting for the house in Boise, Idaho,
where he was born.... If I were God
I'd authorize Celestial Liquid Paper
every seven years to whiten our mistakes:
we should be sorry and live with what we've done
but seven years is long enough and all of us

deserve a visit now and then
to the house where we were born
before everything got written so far wrong.

Stephen Corey

Learning to Live in America

One seldom thinks of Delaware,
yet surely as the Tetons rise
in any painting, starving dogs
like unicorns roam the streets
of Wilmington, and cabbies joust
on freeways no smaller than our own.
None of us knows anyone
who has walked in North Dakota,
but our glove compartments overflow
with maps we've collected, lined for Bismarck.
We must be ready for Missouri—
the European countries it will hold
in silhouette, the soggy issue of *Time*
in a St. Joseph alleyway,
the girl by the river whose breast glistens
from the touch of her lover's tongue.

Belief

for Roland Flint

> *somehow*
> *in between the wood and wine*
> *there will be no separation,*
> *wood dark from wine.*

Because my home is long I read your poem
that night as I walked from bedroom to hallway
to foyer. The light in the corridor
faded toward the front of the house.
Your words on the page grew dim,
so when I reached the black doorway
the last word on the page
was the last I could have read—
as if this were the perfect poem,
its wood and wine in step with my life,
the seamless end shivering my skin
because when the doctor said it was a daughter
I was kneeling by my wife's face,
and for a moment, while I had to wait
for his hands to lift from between her legs,
I was father and not-father, with nothing
but belief to tip me either way,
to show me my new life and my old at once,
with nothing but belief joining
the rooms of every home we walk.

Failure To Be Priests: A Modern Harvest

> *...as a stallion stalwart, very violet-sweet...*
> —Gerard Manley Hopkins

If we do not see the horses fraught with flowers,
the musical fire of invisible hummingbirds,
the graceful, loping gait of tombstones crossing fields,
it is from our stagnant fear of mockery—
our worry to be right, and righteous, and exact—
our failure once again, on waking, to be priests.

We know this globe that could be a mushroom
might not be at all—sprouting fast but scarcely quick
into the far blue air we have named God's face—
so now we find that all we can believe
is so much less than all, is shadowed and shackled
by dark and thinning thought, by chains of flimsy logic
closing off the organ's pipes to still
our outrageous music, our glorious tin-turned-to-golden singing.

Taking the Light Whitely

Certain habits can seem miraculous
in the thoughts of the dispossessed:
to have chosen your own clothing
from stores and then your closet,
to have shaven yet again in the mist
dulling your bathroom mirror—
such are the dreams of the homeless...

I rarely consider my fingers or tongue
until slicing or slamming or burning.
Now, I see how the air outlines the air
in every space where you're not.
I see how we let the ways we caressed
mound like seeds in a bushel basket,
uniform, topping off higher and higher
for as long as we could pour.
I see all those mornings by windows,
on beds nearly overflowing
with movements we made and made, and felt
we watched more closely than we did.
Now, we are a history I work to imagine
into every place we were, a chronicle
no others could even think to restore.
And we are a future, scattered across the country
in the separate strings of houses
we will come to occupy with others—
some for many years.
We do not know them yet; there is nothing
familiar in their rooms or air.
And still, each holds today
what will hold when we've come and gone:

shafts of sun on a thin sill, a pine floor,
a stark wall of whatever color—
one space after another
taking the light whitely,
spot after spot illumined
by that which must touch without touching.

Migration

To this small hill in Mexico
comes every Monarch butterfly alive.
You can lie on the grass and be covered
with hundreds of bright and weightless bodies.
From a short distance off, you will appear
as a shimmering black and orange angel
burning against the hillside. You can think
how the rest of the world is empty
now of this beauty which buries you here.
It will leave for fifty weeks,
but will return in different bodies
to this same place, and will light upon you
if you are here. Can you refuse these rests,
these hair-like legs brushing you until it seems
they could lift your skin into the sky?

Deaf and Mute

Safe beyond the edge of the country
we walk the streets and beaches of this island,
off-season guests holding hands fiercely,
inviting the sparse crowd to know that we are lovers.

An old and very local museum
falls victim to our constant laughter
as we tour its chaotic displays:
Beneath the photo of a 1920's bowling team,
a glass case with one cow's skull,
one rusted shovel, and one tin bucket.
Handwritten cards beside them read,
respectively, "Old," "Very Old," and "Ancient."
Down the hall, a foot-high copy of the *Pietà*
sits atop a case of military medals;
above the Lord, a photograph of the smiling,
monocled comedian, Charles Coburn.

The old deaf curator missed our giggles.
Your breathing and moaning do not pass
beyond this room. On the nightstand
your watchstrap arcs the left lens of my glasses,
both dwarfed by the pink telephone.

And now you sleep curled on your side,
hands tucked beneath your cheek, lips parted.
And I sit watching those lips: everything
they are not saying, all the sense
they cannot make until they touch my skin.
Before today, have we ever heard or said
a single word we could not live without?

Lola Haskins

A Confluence

The clear Ichetucknee fingers into
the dark red Santa Fe,
which carries purity and great cold
downstream
until it is lost in murk of sun
where wrist-thick moccasins ess along
and alligators surface then disappear,
or drag their bellies up the muddy shore.
We have forgotten who we were, young
and eager, kissing through the telephone.
The Suwannee is in no hurry,
has rocked all the humming afternoon.
Now she takes two yarns from a basket
at her side, and with long white needles
begins to knit. The low sun glints
on the tips of her flying. Across her
broad lap, something wonderful begins.

Matanzas

A rod jammed into the sand
the thin line from its tip to the sea
relaxed

and him down the beach
picking up broken angels' wings
with a boy's faith

in what swims in deep water
when suddenly, raptly, his rod bends
and he pounds towards it,

pounds heart-footed
towards what is silver and struggles
in every boy and

flushed, he reels it in.
What next, he never thought. It leaps
and gasps in his hands.

How I Learned

for D'Arcy

For years I made you purple presents.
Mauve blouses, lavender skirts,
fuschia scarves that flowed.
For each occasion, another shade
of bruise, sweet as the fumes of
Daddy's disappearing Buick, achy as
the strokes of tight-lipped Mommy,
brushing my hair. I thought you'd
wear them. I thought they'd become
you, being blonde. But you put them,
all my purple gifts, in one deep drawer.
And now, grown, you take them out.
At first it pains, how new they are.
Then you smile. *Let's give these
away*, you say. And the spring sun
back-lights your hair. You look
like some kind of angel, standing
there in your bedroom, the shine
of what to keep, and what to let go
falling through both our hands.

Uchepas

Tamales plain-steamed then whitened
like a wedding dress, with cream
and queso. A beautiful, simple food.
And not enough.   We want more.

We are cravers of storms and choques
on the highway. We never mind
waiting in the long stopped lines
if at the end there can be some blood.

Forget our lovers. We want
a stranger, shiver deepest at the
hairs on the backs of someone's
hands, who has not touched us yet.

The Prodigy

He was born with the fingerpads of the blind.
By eight he could tell if someone
had been at the piano before him,
and how long before, and who.
Beginning *Für Elise* one November afternoon,
he burst into storms of tears
because his sister had banged
her tuneless anger the night before,
and he felt the bruises still on the keys.

He was born with the ears of a dog.
He could hear his mother's skin decay,
the soft give
as her cheeks sagged just barely more.
Sometimes his face would cloud
because the moan of needles becoming
earth seemed so incomparably sad.
Or brighten. He had heard
the sun come out on the beating feathers
of birds, miles away.

He was born with his life in his hands.
Toddling, he learned the little bells
of Grieg. Then he mastered Mozart's
speech, its ache of clean and brittle
song. Then he learned to follow Bach,
crossing water from calm to flood,
up and down the stepping-stones
of the keys. He would dream
of his piano as if it were flesh.
In a room with a strange instrument
he would walk by it once or twice,
brushing it as if by accident
with his leg, his sleeve.

G.S. Sharat Chandra

Immigrants of Loss

In between the lights
we swallow the open sea,
then zip its back.

Now our body is black molten skin,
its brief, bright twin
shadowing our vanishing acts—

not that we live in the ocean,
half spine, half thread,
our names deep in the throat of waves.

Women sit in their rooms
reading what we wrote
in the lost country of arms.

Above these doors,
dreaming a thousand repetitions,
ghosts brag about abundance,

the swift notion of flesh
on the margin of hollow oars,
holding faint promise.

At the Burning-Ghats

The dead arrive
in carts or on bamboo
prostrate or in postures
held by rope

It's the holy Friday half a dozen gods
were born
the line of souls awaiting deliverance
is long
the pallbearers jockey for positions
or fall asleep
at the feet of their fare

An old man has brought his only son
a young widow revolves around
her lord and master

The Ganges flows gulping bones
here and there a petal of rose or lotus
floats with the ash of the rich

The priests their fee fixed
not by gods but by Trustees
chant standard absolutions
entreating the flames
to levitate each soul
to its proper class in heaven

The chosen burn slowly
the odour of intestines fills the air
as they twist out of their bondages

When the last cadaver is set ablaze
the priests yawn and get up
as if from poker
the night's winnings
tucked into their dhoties

Love Rites

I cut my finger
slicing cucumbers,
I sucked the blood,
she came and kissed
the slices of my hurt,
O my, it felt good.

I cut my finger,
sucked the blood,
I liked the taste.
I wonder now
if I cut another,
would she make haste
to suck it better.

I cut my finger.
It was a bleeding shame
to tell her,
she was gobbling
everything on the plate.
If this be love,
she be vampire,
I be safe bait.

I cut my finger,
looked for a bandaid
which wasn't there
like love when you need it,
so bounteous elsewhere.

I cut my finger
slicing cucumbers,
I got mad and swished it
in the blender,
she asked coyly,

was I cooking a wish
or dishing a murder.

I didn't cut any fingers,
put bandaids over them
just to impress her,
now everyone is doing it.

This is about fingers,
precious love
that ribbons over words
in my written line.
She's wooed by others,
would you be my valentine.

Identities

They bang seals
of embossed words on my passport—
entries, exits.
On the photograph,
a circle of words
slicing my ear
declares who owns me.

On the last page,
there are countries
I cannot enter,
doors that I may open
only with special permission.

I'm claimed by seals
badgered on pages,
injury upon injury,
fresh blues for arrivals,
healed blues for departures,
the slam bang of bureaucracies.

Someday I'll take my duplicate selves,
give up my face,
wear the untouched name,
disappear between doors.
Then they'll mutter in languages
memorized in orphanages
as to whose baggages they carry,
waking from body to body.

Joanne Childers

Tracking Halley's Comet

Although we knew our lives too short for stars
we ventured forth to view their years of light
visible that night. We crossed the flats
and where one finds cross-sections of land-time,
fossils of those lives that moved in strata
of earth drained of the sea, shark's teeth, bleached skulls,
we searched the huge dark window of the sky
to find the comet traveling the heavens
forever and forever. Soon we saw
its little tail that blew and trailed a spray
of sparks across the darkness. It would not
be back again in our time. Only one
of us had lived when last the comet passed
and said she saw it on a far-off hill
back home, its lights performing then with splendor,
its flares that streaked the heavens lighting up
the countryside diminished now. And now
become a child again, the dazzlement
grown dim she looked up from the land-time's prairie
to spot the comet on its bright return,
wanting so to see its light of love,
its hope of grace, its faith that traveled back
like something there forever in the dark.

Garden-Touring with Aunt Mae

We know God by His superfluousness.
—Robinson Jeffers

She does not photograph the faces, secret,
Of tourists as they scurry toward the bus,
Their eyes and mouths concealing who knows what.
Instead Mae aims her camera at the rays

Of sunrise blooms intruding on the gravel,
Attending 8 a.m. Ignoring cows
Like Brahman Rodins; barns calendrical;
Crows that drop from oaks; uprooted trees,

Taproots like spokes; she focuses her lens
On Queen Anne's lace, adjusts her mechanism
Where rampant in a ditch, its efflorescence
Reflects her aging spinster's imagism.

Our tour bus zig-zags east toward noon. Then, as
We grab our scarves, umbrellas, clamber down
To the Driftwood Inn for beer, for seaside vistas,
Aunt passes up the smile of the man

Out front, who sells his cakes to benefit
The parish. Camera in her freckled fist,
She bids me follow her along the street
To find the churchyard. In the rising mist

That shrouds the graves, the pain of man disposed
To perish like cut flowers in the yard,
She woos the spirit of the rambling rose,
Exclaiming all the while, "Thank you, Lord."

Near twilight. I, the more eclectic,
Suggest that Mae record the passing castle,
The candles of the chestnut trees, majestic,

But she prefers the late light on the thistle

Jostling its shadow. Dusky now.
We pull in at the Midland Lodge where Mae
Ignores the sand grains in the porter's eyes,
The eloquence with which he handles keys.

Like Peter at the gate. Instead she fancies
Monkshood pouring forth its purple essence
Beside the door, its cheeky panicles
Sparking her eye as at God's countenance.

Then in a sudden stay I understand
How Mae is flush with the chemistry of life,
As she kneels to the hue and beauty which attend
Creation in the flair above the leaf.

This Reminder

There is this reminder in the kumquats
I pick today in an intimacy
with earth, a faint breeze cooling my sweat
and lifting the dirt-smell from beneath the tree.
There is this feeling that comes back again
so that my thoughts are children picking fruit
in summer, importantly, as if the act obtained
from greater deeds. Then summer days were emblems
of fruitfulness so that I touch the memory
of the grapes on the arbor, blue globes on stems
giving way to ripeness. And the plum tree
with stippled leaves and grandfather pruning
restoring the tree's health, his rusty fingers
deft with the clippers, his tall hat crowning
his shadow. Something in this act that lingers
recalls my dead mother's boiling the plums,
preserving them for summer's fruitful breath
to breathe in me all winter. As her blood thrums
in my veins I pick kumquats now, her youth
and mine merging in loss. There is this reminder
of heat tingling on adolescent skin
as sun fingers the cheeks of ripened pears
and youth passes on in its strength and pain
so that mine and hers become a simulacrum
of all men everywhere. Reaching for fruit
in the orchards of our lives, groping for plums—
the best of what we are and hold as true—
our passion grasping at the world we know,
we savor nourishment, no more, no less
than touching growth like fruit on an old tree,
or one last burst of painful happiness.

Brandon Kershner

Tantrum

Naked, trembling like
a tuning fork, he clutches
and buffets me. His face
is a scrawled howl
of shame and rage.
There's nothing to be done:
he's stumbled on
some Absolute here,
where desire balances
like a grinning egg
high above the world's
stony ground.

                This
is all about power,
I tell myself, cradling
him like a baby with
claws. He's choking
on impossible words,
on some horrible
music his body must
make in its helpless,
fine bones.

                This is about
the wolf he smells on
my breath as I whisper
hush, hush, hush.
God help this house of straw.

Scotoma

Migraine. An orgasm, says the doctor,
        of neurons. Such a gorgeous
vocabulary for the banal

agony I bring him: what is the name
        for the numb hours before
it nestles behind my eyes

when I feel I have forgotten
        something unforgivable?
Aura, he says, the *aura.*

I see a woman gliding in
        my brain, veiled, an annunciation
in an obscure tongue.

Does your wife's face dissolve
        then, he asks, concerned. It does.
Everywhere I look there is no center,

Doctor, there is a swarming hole
        in my sight. I try to read
and see only the margins

of a boiling page. *Scotoma,*
        he announces, delighted. Pascal
saw crystal jungles, pyramids

gleaming everywhere. Hildegard of Bingen
        saw heaven's walls. All *scotoma.*
Hildegard glides in my brain,

a nun on wheels, and whispers something
        medieval about the scintillant
hole in the center of things

into which I am falling
        with these beautiful words for wings
fluttering in the doctor's huge,

hygienic breath. Aura,
        scotoma, and then the pain
to cradle like a child

who will not sleep, Doctor,
        until God speaks to it
some unexpected word.

Responsibilities

I would have saved them except
for the sudden crack that broke underfoot
like thunder, the bridge's yaw and shudder.

Except for the burst hydraulic line, the pilot's
gabble, the slow-rolling fuselage
as a wing-tip sparked against asphalt, then crumpled.

Except for the coked-up crazy at the Jiffy
Mart spraying the aisles of Snickers and Huggies
with white terror, except for the careening

Firebird, except for the split railing,
the slippery step, the charleyhorse fifty
feet out, the rogue cell blossoming,

I would have saved them. These are secret
spells: Do not speak to strangers. Buckle up.
Wash your apples. Learn your number.

Crossing the street, look both ways.
Take my hands. There is always a way,
always the way we forgot to look.

What It Is

lies along the thin
bones of my son's
neck when he watches
us from his own
room. What it is
curled under my brother's
eyes when he shouted
at father in the dark,
breaking voice we never
use.   You cannot watch
what it is except from
the side of your eyes, bending
to pick up socks or to check
a draft under the new
door. I have found its
traces along the cat's spine

and once when you lay
by me like a polite
stranger in a train
pretending sleep, I saw
your body was a phrase
in a long, tedious,
undelivered letter
once meant for me.

Now when it explodes
like a question in my chest
as the razor in my hand
crosses my face, I watch
through the window behind
me in the mirror
the way shadow branches
in the bright hedge.

Dredging

I wrote this poem last year
too shallow. Rick said he nicked his keel,
Rhonda went aground the first time out.
I work nights mostly on the dredge.
It's quiet, except for the heavy, low scrape,
the dull chink of chains rolling out
over the poem. Sometimes
I let it go on while I sleep—
wake up to run out a plumb,
check the bottom silt first thing.
I turn over once on the cot, look
out over the poem toward a few
lights at the edge, think whatever
comes—old lovers, how to get
the rust off my hands. Feel a light,
fishy breeze, imagine I hear music
from somewhere over the chunk, scrape.
I think of Thoreau's line, a man
needs only to be turned around once
with his eyes shut in this world
to be lost, and suddenly
the huge shape looms up in the dark
and I hear bells, bells, a blast
from a funnel the size of Connecticut
and I yell go back go back
I'm not finished yet

P.V. LeForge

Sweater

While others go to parties
or to the movies,
I stay home and sweat.
When people play hockey or tennis,
I sweat watching them.
I sweat on trains, in restaurants.
I sweat in blizzards.
My bed knows it,
so do my clothes;
but when I tell people this
they shy away.
Other people never seem to sweat.
Their clothes remain dry
even on sweltering days,
even in rainstorms.
I put plastic mattress covers on my bed,
but the sweat still seeps through.
Women won't sleep with me.
They're afraid of waking up
floating downstream.
I dream of sweating great torrents
that drown thousands.
It's a habit I can't break,
a cool vice for my hot skin.
My landlady gives me towels for Xmas
and tells me that mine is the only room
in the house not bothered by rats.
Here's my quandary: I want to be liked
but each time I dry my face
or put on a freshly laundered shirt,
my whole body starts to cry.

Anting

When I was 7, I peeked
through a curtain
and watched my mother
placing ants on her clothes
to crawl up her sleeves
and across her bare, painted feet.
I saw her put them down her blouse
and smile.

We had a thick slatboard fence
around our back yard
so neighbors couldn't watch
as my mother held out her arms
and preened like a sparrow.

As the years passed
I tried to ignore those
moving freckles, to pass them off
as little ink stains
or floating cinders
come to rest.
She never spoke to me about the ants
and I never asked.

For parties, Mother would shower
and dress in sheer decolletage
but I'd still imagine those little tunnelings
under that long silk screen
as they made their winding way
up the back of her neck
and into her beehive,
loaded with winter provisions.
I remember that drugged-sensual smile
with which she served the hors d'oeuvres.
She was always picking lint from her dress,
hitching up her slip, scratching a swollen ankle

with the tip of a high-heeled shoe.
Upstairs when she tucked me in
she would pat that bouffant to sleep
and rejoin her guests.

I'm in another city now.
I don't know if my mother
still dances with the ants,
but lately, I've observed
long lines of black workers
inching up my fingers like travelers
who know their way.
At first I was appalled
and flicked them off my skin
and out of my apartment.
But that touch to my fingertips
was tantalizing.
I wanted more.

It's a vice, I know,
but once a month, sometimes twice,
I drive out to an empty field,
bare my skin to the sun,
and spill little tracks of honey
down my arms and toes.
With a drop on each nipple
and behind my ears,
I let them have their way with me.

Those Moments That Make Us Remember We're Alive

Sometimes life stops.
Remember the bovine
between you and the setting sun:
gazing placidly into an inner distance
and chewing on a stream of grass
93 million miles long.
That one scene is all you ever need
to remember of cows.

Think of other times:
a foggy morning on the road
between here and Belle Glade.
The median lines crawl through your wipers
like thick seconds.
Your thermos is warm against your thigh.
An old church bus full of migrants
pulls your eyes off the road.
The driver, bent over,
hitches on another tire.
The others—dark and battered men—
play mumblety-peg by the ditch.
Their knives point to their situation:
part way to the cane fields
and part way home.
For them, life is in limbo;
for you, life stops.

At a public toilet
a scorpion slides across the white
porcelain of the urinal.
You move quickly,
but life stops.
You will see that tail,
like an unsprung switchblade,
forever.

When you held your life like a flaming match
was it any different?
When you taped up that first peso
over the grill,
when you settled your first mortgage,
didn't life give a short pause
and stare at you across the busy counter
before moving off again?

The sun migrates across whatever scenes
death can spare,
and we have many of these small reprieves
living within us.
When we die, will life stop again?
And for who?

The Secret Life of Moles

I used to ride the subway
to the farthest parts of the city.
I discovered routes that were known
to only a secret few:
arthritic travelers with long nails
and dots for eyes
that ate newspaper
and slept on the seats.

I rode till the tracks stopped.
Somewhere outside town
I bought a house
with no stove or furniture.
It was a twin of all the other
houses on the block.
I spent my time picking
at the carpet.
I burned those nappy piles
of fluff for heat.

I quarried the foundation
and stacked rubbled concrete
against the doors.
The unveiled earth
was dark and musty
and I slipped into it like an old lover.

My neighbors did this too.
Through my windows
I saw them, like coal miners
or bank robbers,
stealing outside
with sand in their pockets.

I dug burrows
under my back yard.

I ate tubers
and went on expeditions
to other neighborhoods
where people with long snouts
and sandy whiskers
hung out in bomb shelters
and root cellars.

I covered up my windows with dirt
and learned the secret of moles.
It's not the dark they crave,
it's the digging.

W.C. Morton

River Rats

It's a worse life than most will admit,
eating oysters and mullet
until it's hard to tell the difference
and always remembering the taste and the greasy flesh
of raccoon.
It's hard
to forget the spark in their eyes that fades
when you kill them—
for food, yes
but still you watch them die
whether in a leg trap or an icechest.

It's a harder life than most will admit,
being out in the weather so much
being drunk whenever possible
half-crazy most of the time.
Envy will finally throw you into the sky,
imagining the lives those others lead,
the ones with cars and money and women,
until your mind breaks and you find yourself—
badly beaten behind the Club Two Spot one morning
or maybe just riding naked down the Intracoastal Waterway in your
boat,
shooting at the tourists.

Intimations

There's a lime-green iguana
living under the bridge on Bonita Drive
just past the visitor's gate.
I have watched its image rise above the bamboo
and move across the water.
It hangs upside down and gazes into the canal
past the clouds, the mosquito fish,
concrete,
and its own reflections.

Today I hung from the bridge
by my ankles
and searched the waters.
A stoop-shouldered, balding, pink man,
fingers touching circles on the surfaces of his world,
looked down into the canal and found
it hard to breathe.
The cars sometimes stopped to talk or look
at the pair of sneakers pointed up,
"What are you doing?"
"Crazy fool!"
"Do you need help?"
My sneakers are very quiet—
the cars eventually move on.

There is a ceiling to this surface
with great membranes hanging down,
and there are bottoms deep enough for anyone.
But the ankles grow weak,
head begins to boil,
and I fear I'll fall into the sky
and drown.

In a Tree Stand West of Raleigh

Getting up here is the difficult and dangerous part,
but after I'm strapped on and hanging from the pine,
sweating with the vertigo and exertion of the climb,
it's as quiet as a swallow rising
over a long-abandoned temple,
for a while.

Then the locals' music begins,
and every soprano under an inch takes a part:
the chorus-like crescendo
on the wind-carried melody
as the pine sways in time.

All are suddenly hushed,
as if by some invisible conductor,
leaving only the rustle of a chipmunk
lifting some fallen leaves
and rubbing them together,
as if in applause.

When I look below
a vortex pulls me down
and I must look away—
into some light-tan thickets
or at the sun's purple dappling
on the forest's shoulders
across the cut-over.

I lean back into the tree,
perhaps like Ishmael leaned back into his ship's mast
the first time he lost sight of land
and realized the hunt had begun.

Florida Prelude

Not unlike those Indians
who first saw a white man
and dreamed nightmares of ochre skies,
of big wind
and built
huge piles of oyster shells,
we too sometimes see ourselves,
riding off cliffs.

In this South,
it is all so much armor
that makes it difficult to walk,
and survival a possibility.
We mime that large reptile
this land is known for—
we say to ourselves,
"Wait a million years;
things will improve"—
and learn patience.

Or we mime that fish
this land is known for,
that worries the tourists
at the oceanside,
and we display our appetites
our own furies—
and learn hate.

We live our own sad myths down here.
We hear the wind blowing,
down here.

Edmund Skellings

Incantation

I keep coming to this chair
Today. Back and forth between
The ficus tree trailing aerial roots
Outside, and this chair.

Back and forth between
The tame wood and the free.

I am a hammock hung to the winds.
I am a sail today.
I strain as hard as I can and then
Go back to the measured tread again.

What can I start? My pencil breaks.
The ficus creaks with the breeze.
The chair creaks with my weight.

Axes, I threaten. I shall kindle
Some kind of blaze. You shall be
Food for fire if not thought.

The empty tree whispers of singing birds.
The empty chair is silent with its dead.

More, I shout, to the arching rafters.
The door shudders on its jambs.
The shelves under the books stiffen.
The table offers coffee.

Oh God, I hear the forests falling.
Timbers moan in the holds of the ships.
Spars sing in the wings of planes.

All the toboggans in the hills are rushing,
Skis are hissing,
The great woods of the world are howling.

The pines of the walls encircle me.
The polished years are shining like brown bones.
I sink into the chair.
The tree enters the house.

Now all the druids are dancing.

Heartwood

You chopped the tree down though it held my house
And tore away the brush and cleared a court.
Too young to play, I loved to watch the sport,
So if it cost my house I felt no loss.

From a rickety ladder at net height
The ball was like my globe at school, but white.
I didn't know the rules. It was my game
To see who kept the ball longest in air,
Patting my leather world with his strong hands.
But when it stayed so long I thought it tame,
Someone would slip and miss it bouncing, or
Somebody near the net would thump it down.

Then the turtle came. And volleyball
Raised no more dust in air than catching him.
Two feet across, at least six inches tall,
He eyed the ring of feet, looked for a place to swim,
And finding none, pulled in his legs and tail.
The head stayed part way out. His leather back
Was brown, but stitched and round, like half the ball.

"Ride 'im, Romey!" And for a little while
You, Father, stood astride half of my globe,
Taller than everyone. O, what a smile!

"There is a story that if you set flame
Beneath a turtle's belly he will crawl
Out of his shell," one of the big men said.
"I wonder if he would?" "Can't ever tell!"

You carried oily rags from the garage
And rolled the turtle on them with a stick

And once it was begun the test was quick.
A match was struck, and caught in seas of fire
The turtle tried to dig down to his mud.

Whoever told the story was a liar.

A summer of scrapes, and bitter bruises, too.
Always your voice to flinch me, "You won't die!"
So I did all a boy can ever do.
I ran away from laughing gods to cry.

It was a wicked summer I recall.
More than a turtle died within his shell
The day house tree and legend fell.

The Leningrad Writers Conference 1942

for Yevgeny Yevtushenko

The starved had reached one thousand a day
With the temperature thirty below zero
And the writers had to burn their chairs
But they did meet and hold their conference.

Zhenia, tonight I watched the old films
Of that Hero City holding out holding out
Holding out under months of shells falling
On homes with thick frost on the inner windows

And I thought of our first meeting in Alaska
With all the writers gathered at the college
And how we talked of poetry half the night
While outside the cold and the blackness waited

Zhenia, tonight I sit writing in Florida
Sipping from the simple white of cold milk
While the long breath of the air cooler
Settles over my shoulder like a shawl

And I hardly know what I am trying to say
Only that somehow the boiling heart
As well as the frozen bone must be held back
By poets who must ever keep their conference

Eugenie Nable

The Elephant Mother and Her Baby at the Tampa Carnival

Chained two legs each to the shopping center sign,
    you do not flinch at the highway cars with their
    bulging insect eyes, but do a dance of sway and rock,
    back and forth, loose long noses rubbery and heavy.

Last week I read in the news that one of your tribe
    ramped on her trainer then squashed him against the wall
    with her big head, that she did not crush his skull
    into the concrete with either of her forefeet.

After they shot her for killing a human,
    someone noticed a pale fungus growing
    on the bottoms of her feet which were swollen
    and oozy, ragged with torn craters of open flesh.

I had thought that elephant feet could feel no pain,
    those arched toenails melding into hard hooves,
    tough, something besides tender.
Inside circus tents when I was little,
    I never did ponder those flexible ankles and soles molding
    to the giant balls in the centers of the three rings.

I never knew you could undulate your great toes
    so precisely bundled and wrapped onto tree sized legs,
    walking forever barefoot on oil and acid and glass,
    walking forever barefoot into metal railroad cars,
    walking forever barefoot on miles of freezing concrete,

    not on a clean river bottom, not on a real jungle floor,
    not on ocean sand, not on plains, not much on natural dirt.

I step closer to you who are the mother
    knowing that pain can make anger and danger.
My left hand strokes your huge heart-shaped face,
    humped and crowned with bristly red hairs.

Intimate as a memory you bend toward me
    and press your brow against my small mammal body,
    brushing your lower loose lip across the back of my right hand
    tickling my skin with your downy beard.

The warm muscles of your trunks twine about my arms and thighs
    to scoop the pomegranates, apples, oranges, and avocados
        I offer.
You push the fruit into diamond-shaped mouths the color of
    bubblegum
    and probe the pink folds around the huge molars for
        remnants of food.

As you crunch whole avocados, I make up songs about past times
    when you swam the straights of Ceylon with your clan,
    when you bulbed from your two-year womb into salty water
    up into the air where your grandmother and aunty pulled you.
Do you remember the pungent earth you traveled to?
Do you remember the succulent leaves above you?
Do you remember your elephant life in the forest?

The carneys stare our way and watch me laugh and babble
    and you just sniff me with those fingertip snouts that
    suck against my eyes, my cheeks, my nostrils, the palms
    of my hands and my crotch, your sweet breathing seeking
    more oranges, and searching the source of my smells.

Clutching a bag of Purina Horse Chow, a grizzly-skinned trainer
    barks at me "She won't hardly touch meat unless she's starvin'.
    She loves all this fruit you're givin' her, though it's gonna
        make her fart

and the marks might not like that!" Saliva explodes from
    his laughter.

I look down at your supple feet
    pushing on the asphalt in Tampa
    where I leave you
    where you leave me
    creatured with these orange breath kisses,
    the last one lingering, suckled on my forehead, exact and sticky.

The Fish Man

...to breathe in any way but like a fish is dangerous
—Joseph Barth

He says "You remind me
of a woman I knew whose
lines were perfectly
cast for the part, who
reeled me with longing
into the night," yet
how can he see me when
he smothers me so close?

What does he see through
his tangled vision?

Did he ever see her,
the ex-ex girlfriend
lying beneath him
ascending above him
like a shiny lure?

I recede and am not myself
but the Indian squaw fixed
on the Land O'Lakes butter
carton who holds her own
image, who holds another,
each one swallowing the other
into illimitable distance.

Am I his x-rated heart flick
in which anybody is the star?

A star. Finite and measurable
whose light dissociates from
its source, burns on the
surface of the sky.

He says "I won't be
any woman's fish to be
baited and hooked by a glimmer."

I say "Your eyes bulge.
Where are these hooks,
lines and sinkers?"

He gapes at me. I hold myself.
He blinks. I fade slowly
into darkness saying "If
a man is afraid of a hook,
then he must live otherwise;
down in some smooth lake."

A Late Night Telegram to Dr. Christiaan Barnard

Dear Christiaan, Transplanter of Hearts,
Gather your staff and come quickly—the word is out
that you have been asked to perform the first human head
   transplant.

You've come a long way since 1967
and all those unanesthetized chimpanzees
having their hearts cut out before their open eyes.

And now you've got to get to my house.
My bedroom is filling up with transplant candidates who are
arriving here for their operation—silent volunteers stepping from
my closet, headless bodies holding talking heads and climbing
   through my window.
Really, this is just too much.

At least a hundred Rhesus monkeys, each with a thorny necklace of
stitches, scramble and leap from wall to wall in search of their
original bodies. They are the living proof that head transplants do
   come true.
One just landed on Mary Queen of Scots who sits on my bed
cradling her head in one arm and rattling the newspaper at me with
   the other:

SHOULD THE DECAPITATED BE MADE WHOLE?

The story reads that you have been offered 250 million American
dollars to perform the first human head transplant and that you
   refuse to collaborate...
"The idea is immoral, lacks ethics, is impractical and of dubious
legality," you tell the reporters, but Dr. Barnard, you can't turn
   your back on this.
You've got to fix these people up so they'll get out of my room, out
   of my life.

I cannot have John the Baptist's holy head smiling his sorrow at me
every time I reach for my comb or deodorant. He simply requests
that you hook him up with this gourmet cook standing next to the
 dresser, a cleaver in his hand.
John wants to forget the drunken decree, the dying, and how his
ragged neck rested on that silver platter draped with scarlet silk
 before Herod and Salome....

These goddam monkeys! I'm going mad, Christiaan.

Now what. Who? Pushed onto the subway rails and lost his head?
And who is this one singing Celtic ballads? Of course, of course, it's
that darling hero, Great Bran, once taller than a Druid stone, his
huge head toppled and chunked down on top of his land's high cliff
to sing and speak forever; so Barnard, you're to connect the head of
Bran to that startled subway heart and body and we will witness the
new-age man strolling down Madison Avenue, prophesying and
yodeling, tingling the genes of latter day Celts who will think this
overblown face is papier mache, some Disneyworld escapee who
parades about in that perplexed and dissociated New Yorker body.

You say the whole thing lacks ethics, is impractical, but my god,
Barnard, what am I to do? Loosen up those arthritic hands and
 operate.
How can I restore every son of Medea, every Anne Boleyn,
every head hacker's victim, or Holofernes who tumbles from my
 closet?

OK, OK, as for morals and legality, consider Medusa here
(safely inside the cat carrier)—attach her writhing head to that
Florida truckdriver's body leaning against the wall in the corner (his
head last seen after the wreck, rolling down Highway 50 and
snatched up by a Pine Hills biker who roared off to Ocoee on his
 leopard-skin chopper).

Put a pair of shades on Medusa, wrap her snakes in pink foam
curlers and see how well she drives that rig of Mexican produce
 from Orlando to Atlanta.

Thankful for a job, she'll never go on strike—surely a legal and
moral life after the severance of head from heart and the merging of
    such strangers.

So, please, Christiaan Barnard, come right away.
I've cleared the kitchen table and put water on to boil.
You must get here immediately—the monkeys are tearing up the
place and I cannot stand these chattering heads and yearning bodies
    much longer.
Every one is here waiting for you.

Nancy Powell Rousseau

J. Ford in the Water Hyacinths

It wasn't the rats he feared
nor snakes that dropped from Banyan trees
to hunt cracks in his floor
but crossing the wide canal
in a one-oared skiff to get the mail
when he saw the hyacinths gathering,
long matted hairs reaching down
to root in mud. Day after day
they bobbed lilac
and watched him pass.

He was crossing at dusk,
hyacinths as far as he could see
when the squall blew in,
broke huge clumps loose
that rushed him, spun him around
then swept him broadside
till he was pinned in mid-canal.
Then they folded slowly over his boat.

He tied a handkerchief to the oar
for signal, put the mail in his hat
and eased out onto the floating darkness.
On knees and forearms, palms flat
till an arm sank through
and he changed course. Never mind
what suns its dank self here by daylight
or what lines the shore—inch forward.
Wait for lightning. Fifty yards, no more.
Think of the bank.

Cherry Hammock

When cows gather in the lot at milking time,
click horns, nudge, bulging udders greedy
for relief—hungry for the sound of iron stanchions
clanging shut, for citrus pulp and grain,
a few always remain far at pasture
hiding ankle-deep in ponds to chew their cuds.
It's a rare cow whose brain sparks long enough
to lead her to real cover, but Cherry was one—
a Guernsey who yielded five gallons a day
when you could find her.

Her refuge was the one place
even the horses were scared of
for every crawling thing sought the high ground
of the hammock in the rainy season—blue runners,
diamondbacks, indigoes—coachwhips hung from
mahogany trees, waiting for frogs and rodents.

She would hear you coming
look up from tender shoots
and lead you deeper and deeper into hardwoods
where the biggest spiders threw out their nets.
If you gave chase and hit a web
a Golden Silk big as your face
would run down your back
faster than any horse could move.

When buzzards circle and a cow is missing
you've got no choice
even if it means Cherry Hammock.
If your horse shies as he nears
jump off, jerk the reins till he knows
you mean business, then ride him on in there

where little moves. Only the vultures overhead,
flies that crawl through draining nostrils,
buzzing dark around her eyes, and the dead
drifting smell of a bloated carcass
wedged between two cabbage palms.

Seminole Indian Jacket

Each morning our school bus passed the spot
palmetto roots smoldered,
another cabbage palm was gone.
Scrap lumber started to appear
and stacked itself piece by piece
before dawn. We rode by
and watched for ghosts or gypsies.
Then an omen—a cur dog
tied to a stump.

And just-like-that, there they were,
stacking concrete blocks in hurried rows—Seminoles!
Five of them, dressed in funny clothes. The old one
wore her hair like a hat. We'd seen her
before, down by the marina
under a thatched roof, near the 'gator pen,
sewing for tourists on her treadle machine.
Now her granddaughters
rode our bus to school.

We looked at them hard.
The older one, Dorthea, never raised her eyes
but Sally did once, long enough
to see the older boys leer—
Only my brother smiled. For weeks
it went that way. No one ever
saw them talking, but when he looked at her
she almost smiled, and we all knew.
We kept the silence, hoping Jimmy Stewart
would claim his Sonseeahray
and take her to the bridal tent
where the Princess, draped in white buckskin
brown shoulders bare
would wrap her arms around him
and finally smile.

He found the jacket one early morning
placed in a Melaleuca tree
by the path to the barn. Each strip
of color lit his face like nothing
I had seen—Snowy Egrets
waded in clear water. Green corn
grew. Coots moved through saw grass
and Purple Gallinules walked lily pads to shore
where amber orchids bloomed wild in the trees
and gray moss blew in the wind.

The putting on of it
was a ceremony. He stood tall
facing his mirror, one arm
in the sleeve, when he felt the weight
of the jacket, and realized
it wasn't free.

My brother didn't smile much after that,
the girls no longer rode the bus.
One morning when we passed
the house was gone. People said
it was just like damned Indians
the way they'd torn it down, block by block
and moved it with them
back to the reservation.

He never wore the jacket.
Our mother cut it up
and made it into pillows for the couch.
When people came to visit
they vowed they'd never seen
such cleverness.

They Write From Great Distances

She writes about the weather, ceaseless rain,
the power of water. Whales wheeze
in Silver Bay, salmon die upriver.
She says she's happy.
She's gotten it together—
she doesn't mention her biker lover.

He's building a pick-up
from a hearse he calls El Condor.
He can't take the humidity
he's moving north come Spring.
He'll soon send her belongings
he's low on money. He doesn't mention
what she's already heard—

That he came home bourbon drunk one day
to find a man trespassing
uprooting vegetables
she'd planted last May—
brittle cucumber vines, shriveled tomatoes
cilantro gone to seed. That he cursed
the man and ran him off
then went inside, arms flailing
muttering something
about respect, something
about Wife's garden.

Sam Harrison

A Poem about ~~Substance~~ Sustenance Spaniels

Once, just for the fun of it,
moved by the infinite promise
of a cold Fall afternoon,
we walked through a mansion
empty and for sale on the Hudson,
high on a grand bluff.
There were parquet floors
and wainscot paneling
throughout; the land surrounding tiered
like Chinese steppes;
a barely grassed tennis court
on the last level before
a hundred-foot drop to the river,
the wishful world, the Mongol hordes.

"I grew up here," I said,
as honey sunlight poured
through leaded glass.

"It's been in my family for years,"
my wife said, pointing
to a small quadrangle of light.
"The dog used to sleep over there."

Isle of Flowers

The Last Great Invention

I never told you how I wanted to take out
The ceiling in the living room, build
A loft and library in the attic above
With ladder and railing; install
A skylight on the southern slope
Of the little house we never should have left,
But upward mobile, felt compelled to.
Or of the window boxes to be built
Off kitchen and dining room that in the
Iridescent, verdant Springs to come
Would fill with flowers and the rooms
Themselves with a fragile, corporal light
Which, upon entering, could stop you cold,
But gently, like a lover's hand.

As family grew we might have closed in
The car port, put up Bahamian shutters
Against August when cicadas drone
And the air is wet wool; there was room,
We should have managed.
                              I remember rains
From the front porch gushing through oaks
With a sound like the beginning of the world.

Things' potentials go unmet, stuffed back in
Some closet like a wide tie
In the mad dash for something better,
Something bigger.
And what I am believing, oddly,
Sleepless here beside you on another warm night,
Is that the bicycle was the last great invention,
Everything since being part madness, part
Exuberance; that just because we know how
Doesn't mean we should; that some limitation,

Some saying of when,
Like a trimmed viburnum hedge, is better
Than no limitation at all, and that I could have
Made the wiring last another thirty years.

Air Waves

Havana was virtually next door
when I pressed the small
transistor set to my ear,
something akin to placing
a glass against the wall
to eavesdrop on the neighbors.
The wall was the Gulf of Mexico,
vast, black, and horizontal
conductor of Spanish,
the apartment next door alive
with Latin rhythms, static,
and rapid, cigar-mellowed monologues.
I slept with the radio
between my ear and pillow,
and when I woke in the night,
two, three times, it was
to the somehow comforting sound
of that continuous party.
I dreamed Havana, the boulevard,
the acacia trees in the rain,
someone saying, hey,
turn up the radio.

And then the music stopped.
Not long, a few hours,
one night, at most. There was
the great silence of the Gulf
between us, tentative, uncertain.
And when my neighbors talked again
the voice was a strident harangue,
as if some guest, lampshade on head,
turned mean with drink,
had silenced all the revelers
with what was really wrong
inside of him: the Gulf between us.
When again the same music played

it was sad. I remember
wondering about that. It is like
me telling you, I am in pain,
and you hearing, I want to hurt you.
All my life I have been dreaming
Havana, the boulevard,
the acacia trees in the rain,
someone saying, hey,
turn up the radio.

A Laundromat in Mt. Kisco

He watches her,
reading in a chair
by the window; intense,
absorbed and distant;
a thick book whose title
he cannot see. It is late
afternoon and strange
for her to be this still
this close to dinner,
but there is something
about the coldness of the air,
about the sharpness of the leaves
in the low-angled light, the
monumental solitude
that make this the place to be

for now. Outside,
three birds with burning breasts
descend to a wire.

Nor can he move, leaning
in a doorway, stilled
by this simplest of moments,
his hands forgotten, misplaced
somewhere in air
between tasks.
For he is seeing her
in another time, against
another window, another winter;
clothes chasing round in the dryer
like otters, a first snow wet
on the lettered glass and in
the empty street,
between dreams
when they were very young.

Yvonne Sapia

Fertile Crescent

The shallow arms of the river caress my house.
I am the washerwoman pounding
a futile vision against the rocks.
I wash my clothes in the river's importance.

I've seen dark men walk the banks
of this river. They have waited in moonlight
drenched in that sound of water,
shoulders up against the cold currents.

The lizards have made violent love
by the river beneath a brief sun.
I've watched the perfect lovers
rolling on their green, jagged backs.

The river carries ceremonies and dreams.
In the night I draw a swollen moon
into my mouth and turn
to the river going under.

Into the black offering I fall like a millstone;
into forgetfulness I go further down.
The ocean celebrates my coming
with the vernacular of sea gulls.

The Exile Tree

para los balseros

I

The priest helps the child light one candle in
memory of her mother and father who
disappear in the Atlantic Ocean.
The wick burns. She notices Christ's blue
eyes. He is sad and holds His heart. She too
is sad. The single candle would have been
a great sun lighting her way from home to
America. (The candle lights her mother's skin.
The candle lights her father's black eyes. The
candlelight flickers at stars, like the stars
in the sharks' deadly eyes, the school not far
from the raft of lost refugees.) — *"Habla
Español, niña?"* the priest asks. *"Habla
Inglés?"* The girl stares at the altar.

II

She's drawn by the golden greatness of it,
the priest whispers, only to himself. When
he was a young boy, wild and passionate,
the sight of the crossed man suspended in
another time, left to bleed to death, thin
and exiled from other men, caused a fit
of tears and hopeful dreams of saving
Christ from dying in His own blood and spit.
And in each dream he failed to bring Him down
alive from the exile tree. The priest chose
to accept the belief system, a rose
with thorns. — Thus, he endures this night. No sound
emerges from the dark-skinned girl who's bound
to remember and genuflect alone.

III

She remembers being carried asleep
in her mother's arms to a shore of dreams
and sharp rocks and stars. Her father's voice, deep
and grave, speaks to the waves. His flashlight beams
out into the many moist eyes that seem
to stare back from the rough water. They keep
circling the small raft. She hears the first scream
in the dark drink, the first desperate leap
of the hull collapsing like an empire
to the surface. And before dawn a storm
cracks open the sky with lightning and born
is a beast revolving below. Tired
and cold, her father shouts, "I won't stay there.
Odio ese país," raising his arms.

IV

Suddenly blurred, her gray father falls out
of the raft. He flies like a man who has
to leap into the rain for his home route
or make his way to heaven. Disguised as
a freed spirit seeking the correct place
to leave his body, he resurrects, shouts.
Light in his hand briefly shines on chaos:
blank eyes of the ocean, unending doubt
of survival, last attempts to be saved.
Her mother's wail is unlike any cry
heard by presidents or ministers. Cry
of thunder meets its equal as she raves.
Clutching her child like a good book she saves,
she watches her husband drift off to die.

V

The old priest prays for this perilous world
where paradise unravels one green thread
at a time. "Blessed are the young, the old,
the godless, the godful. Blessed the dead,
the living, the ones who live as if dead."
With no voice to share, she sits still. A girl
is a kingdom no priest can save. She's led
by the voice only she hears in the whirl
of a raft out of control, lost at sea,
where grief begins to struggle one morning
with inevitability. — Floating
like a dead fish in the sun, her raft, free
and directionless, is slapped out of sleep
by cruelty. In waves, something's worth saving.

VI

The mother anoints her child's head and lips
with what fresh water remains to journey
to freedom. Then she cups her hand and dips
into the ocean. She drinks deep salty
tears of the drowned. Her dark bucket body
overflows with their loss. While two suns rip
apart the sky, she talks in her sleep, free
at last in delirium and eclipse
of real things with bad dreams. There are mermaids
ahead, she insists, her gaze lifted to
the imaginary rocks on the blue
horizon sprawling like a line that fades
in the distance, fooling the unaided
eye into believing what is untrue.

VII

A third sun collapses into the sea.
Her mother has not moved or opened her
swollen eyes since last night. The good life she
gave her needs to be repaid. She holds her,
she kisses her, sleeps in her cold arms. Terror
is alive in the dark. Home is only
this nothingness she slides through. Her father,
her aunt and uncle — were they ever free?
Did they too climb the exile tree and reach
for their destinies? Her mother is gone
now, but she cannot let go. She is gone.
They are gone... they are gone. She drifts to search
again and again and thinks of the church
where the dead are praised and burials are done.

VIII

Beneath a sabal palm the raft appears,
lodged in sand and debris forming a vein
along the shoreline near the South Beach pier.
Asleep, the little refugee remains
in the dead woman's arms. A man walking
his dog finds them both, and when the girl hears
the barking, she opens her eyes and trains
her sight up to the swaying fronds that steer
safely across the blue Miami sky. —
Who is she? Will she ever speak? The priest
gazes at the orphaned child. She at least
may live free and one day tell her story
to those besides the exiled man crucified,
to those whose small dark rafts make their way west.

Parts of the Verb "To Be"

am

In silence you run
through the dark woods,
sparks of sun lighting the way.
Trees disappear behind you.
They call your name.

is

Spring pours down.
Your house is a cold bone.
The cats chase and run
to warm themselves.
You drink coffee and rain.

are

In a dark room
you dream wind
shoves the fences down.
Before dawn
you fail to rebuild them.

was

You awake to a perilous world.
The perfect places
rest with your good hand.
Last night
you cut off your bad hand.

were

Her name closes a letter.
The day she goes away
is the day you disappear.
You must find a place
to leave your body.

Hal Shows

Camellias

Out late, in quickening cold far from your own neighborhood, you kneel at the hedge to watch.

Under a bare light the woman is setting her table, stretching to reach a thick blue bowl from a shelf. A man's shirt rides high the curve of her naked hip. She's smiling. She pushes hair out of her face with her free wrist, and the man is suddenly there, his mouth brushing her ear, their foreheads touching. What does he say?

A moment ago the car in the drive next door growled and turned over. You dropped to your knees. Into the road the big headlights swung wide, glared on the stop sign at the corner, turned out of your life. Finally your heart drowned the hum of the motor, and you knelt in the dense, animate shade living things cast at night, safe and ashamed... you thought of leaving...

But over your head the air was full of camellias, heavy, blush-blue flowers hanging on stems close to your hair, and you wanted to touch them.

Sonnet

Outside Dooley's Honest Irish Bar and Grill
Death rattled, firms revved up and fiercely rowed.
Fat contracts abounded; cross-land, farmers,
frightened and famished, swiftly converted the plough.
In Washington Park two truants tied a leash
to a puppydog's tail and dashed him against a wall.
The media frowned, but the lads themselves were proud,
and soon enlisted, eyeing some foreign beach.
Alas! They came home blinded, muttering aloud,
a lot less tall. And that, as they say, was all...
Except we should toast the moneymongering men
who choked the streets to cheer such heroes home
to hovels, rattling sabres, raising glasses
and tossing bones: may they live long, and alone.

Ode on a Train

On the slow diretto south of Rome
the widow in the window seat
turned in her sleep,
draped her arm over mine,
then dragged it up
until her rough palm
gripped my forearm tight.
I could feel her wedding band
against my skin. Then she woke.
She blinked, and got up quickly,
lighting a cigarette as she left the compartment.

I wonder who she thought I was?
Father, husband, lover, son?
Out in the corridor
she holds the metal handle
of the sliding window
with one hand
and flicks ash
into the wind with the other.

This is an old woman, Valerie.
What do you reach for in your dreams?
You hide behind the oldest face
of the moon, hag-goddess
of childbirth and anesthesia,
you shrink on the narrowing ribbon of track
until you are small enough to be everywhere
  at once,
until you become the air I breathe.

I remember your hands.
As the memory of wheat
in shivering rows
touches a fallow field,

only its barbed wire going to seed,
they touch me across time;
they play.

So I wait for you, moving.

Laurence Donovan

Dog Island IV

By day the quick willets
Print the moment
In the sluiced-over sand.
On pipecleaner legs
They peck at surf's edge,
Withdrawing and advancing
With the waves' erasures.
Dimmer white against white,
Their pale negative's
An old sketch of creation.

By night the grackles come down
For the crumbs we put out
On the balcony railing.
They approach from afar
In cartoonish transitions,
Hopping nearer and nearer
Through the soughing pines
To the final dark swoop
And quick flight away,
Crumbs dripping from beak.

The males are grand,
Although shifty and baleful,
And even sardonic
With that one beady eye
(Taken from Poe)
That is meant to transfix:
They bide in near branches,
Their stark silhouettes
Cut in black arcs.

The females are smaller,
Quicker, less fearful,
And impatient to feed:
They come in for the crumbs,
Hop and peck, hop and peck,
In fluttery incisive
Stabs from the air,
Scratching swift glyphs,
Humorous inkings,
Against the lineage,
Pale, of the pines.

Dog Island IX

Jolting down the shell-tamped dirt road
In golf-cart or jalopy, with their rusted-
Out and salt-bitten, cracked-paint exteriors,
Past the platformed spidering beach house
Of the famous golf pro, whose manicured greens
Have dwindled here into a barbarous
Opposite, not velveteen cupping its tidy traps
But gorse and barbed thicket and dune pine
Seizing against the wind the long patches
Of sand; past the single double-decked inn
And the garbage dump under its thrumming flies;
Down the slowcurving spine of the island
To the swampy woods at the western end
Where St. George lies hazy on the near horizon;

Or walking in the sand, eyes out for snakes,
On road- or beach-side of swept-up dunes,
Combed smooth or crumbling in sea and wind,
With long filaments of stubbled vine fingering down
To moist clumps of seaweed lying in lines
Parallel to the water: eyes down or drawn out to
The Gulf under its eye-dazzling sky, pale
Blue or blindingly white as sheet metal; past
Remnants of pierwalks, lines of descending
Stakes in the sand, rotting wooden markers
Whose decks have flown into the whorl of the storm;
Walking like Crusoe on his old island,
Hushed in that monotone, the surf's sibilant whisper,
The curlew's soundless patter, the shellpop underfoot.

The Traveler

I may have arrived just in time to save you the trouble
Of traveling, going out there among the seascapes
And the leaning statues and the other travelers
Looking, or pausing for breath, seated on their great valises
In the smoky stations, muffled, staticky voices overhead
Issuing crisp instructions like starched Eumenides,
Or walking once more in cities quite like their own,
Looking, pausing here and there to buy a postcard.
I may be able to tell you, having been everywhere,
Of Etrurian cabbages and kings and the grinning mummies
Being hoisted around in their palanquins and
The water sluicing down through angels paralyzed in stone
And signs of mistral off Capri, or that dead place
Birds cannot fly over where is the entrance to hell.
Do not go, I urge you, I beseech you. Dim caves
Of night and the blinding gestures of day are all
That lie out there, which have seared and darkened
The face you see before you. Wander within the album
Of yourself, as I have done, surely this should be
Enough for you, such wonders, such wastes are there:
The seagulls shriek behind your ears, forests flicker
Under your eyes, and in your heart the visage
Of an alien art lifts mammothly its marble, telling
You nothing new. My friend, the journey's been done
Long ago. Stay here for now. Listen to me.

Donald Justice

A Winter Ode to the Old Men of Lummus Park, Miami, Florida

Risen from rented rooms, old ghosts
Come back to haunt our parks by day,
They creep up Fifth Street through the crowd,
Unseeing and almost unseen,
Halting before the shops for breath,
Still proud, pretending to admire
The fat hens dressed and hung for flies
There, or perhaps the lone, dead fern
Dressing the window of a small
Hotel. Winter has blown them south—
How many? Twelve in Lummus Park
I count now, shivering where they stand,
A little thicket of thin trees,
And more on benches turning with
The sun, wan heliotropes, all day.

O you who wear against the breast
The torturous flannel undervest
Winter and summer, yet are cold,
Poor cracked thermometers stuck now
At zero everlastingly,
Old men, bent like your walking sticks
As with the pressure of some hand,
Surely we must have thought you strong
To lean on you so hard, so long!

Variations on a Text by Vallejo

Me moriré en París con aguacero...

I will die in Miami in the sun,
On a day when the sun is very bright,
A day like the days I remember, a day like the other days,
A day that nobody knows or remembers yet,
And the sun will be bright then on the dark glasses of strangers
And in the eyes of a few friends from my childhood
And of the surviving cousins by the graveside,
While the diggers, standing apart, in the still shade of the palms,
Rest on their shovels, and smoke,
Speaking in Spanish softly, out of respect.

I think it will be on a Sunday like today,
Except that the sun will be out, the rain will have stopped,
And the wind that today made all the little shrubs kneel down;
And I think it will be a Sunday because today,
When I took out this paper and began to write,
Never before had anything looked so blank,
My life, these words, the paper, the gray Sunday;
And my dog, quivering under a table because of the storm,
Looked up at me, not understanding,
And my son read on without speaking, and my wife slept.

Donald Justice is dead. One Sunday the sun came out,
It shone on the bay, it shone on the white buildings,
The cars moved down the street slowly as always, so many,
Some with their headlights on in spite of the sun,
And after a while the diggers with their shovels
Walked back to the graveside through the sunlight,
And one of them put his blade into the earth
To lift a few clods of dirt, the black marl of Miami,
And scattered the dirt, and spat,
Turning away abruptly, out of respect.

David Kirby

The King Is Dead

The woman who hands me my dry cleaning
   is red-eyed and red-faced, and I think, Jeez,
she's going to hurt herself
   if she doesn't stop trying so hard not to cry,
so I say, "Hold on, it can't be that bad,"
   and she drops my slacks and blazer
on the counter and puts her hands
   over her face and says, "Oh, boo-hoo! BOO-HOO!
The kang is dead, the kang is dead!"
   and the woman behind her
looks at me and silently mouths the word, "Elvis,"

and I, God help me, say, "So?" to myself,
   or at least I hope it was to myself
because I don't like to hurt people's feelings,
   but Elvis had always seemed like
the biggest fake in the world to me:
   my racist cousins who lived in the sticks
would sob their mascara off every time
   an Elvis song came on the radio,
but I figured, Forget it: the only good music
   was not the music Elvis made but the music
Elvis listened to and then watered down

so that white people could stand to be around it,
   and here I'm referring to the kinds of songs
being sung at the same time by Rufus Thomas,
   Irma Thomas, Carla Thomas, Otis Redding,
Barrett Strong, and Doris Troy. Chuck Berry.
   Little Richard. Aretha Franklin. Fontella Bass.
Elvis had already lost me in December 1954

with that false start to "Milkcow Blues Boogie"
("Hold it, fellas. That don't move. Let's get
  real, real gone."); besides, Georges Braque
said that in art there is only one thing

that counts, the thing you can't explain,
  and there was nothing you couldn't explain
about Elvis. Also, anybody who had the Jordanaires
for a back-up group.... Meanwhile,
what about Rufus, Irma, Carla and company?
  Item: I am sitting in the breakfast room of a hotel
in Colmar, in France, having come to see
  the Isenheim Altarpiece of Matthias Grünewald,
and as I break and butter my roll,
  "Good Golly Miss Molly" comes on the radio,
and the most staid Germans, the most dour Swedes,

the most cynical French smile and wiggle
  their shoulders and sort of bop their coffee cups
around their saucers as Richard makes them
  ting-a-ling-a-ling, good golly! Sure like to ball!
Item: in the bootheel of Italy, I am walking out
  of the castle of Otranto (yes, there really is one,
though Horace Walpole never saw it) and hear
James Brown singing it's a man's world and he's LOST!
in the wilderness and he's LOST! in the emptiness,
  and I glance sideways to see that, like me,
my fellow travelers are LOST! in those big chords,

jerking to a halt every time they get LOST!
  and then almost crawling through the heat and the sun
until the next time their spines stiffen and
  they're LOST! in the song and in James Brown's voice,
because, yes, rhythm and blues is like Deutschland,
  it's *über alles*, whereas Elvis would be a dim memory
to most people were it not for the *Weekly World News*
  and those crappy oldie stations that people listen to
so they can find out what they missed
  back when they were too busy painting signs for
their pro-segregation rallies to listen to the radio.

Isle of Flowers

But my personal favorites always were
  and always will be the crooners and balladeers,
the great soul men in their jewelry and shiny suits:
Mr. Solomon Burke, Mr. Chuck Jackson, Mr. Bobby Bland,
Mr. Jerry Butler, Mr. Tyrone Davis (whom I spent
  forty dollars to see once, even though he did
a ten-minute set and said, "Thank you very much,
  you've been wonderful"), and, above these and every other,
the real king, the one and only, the late great
  Mr. Sam Cooke. These gentlemen were way beyond cool.
Also, they had what I wanted. No, not women: audiences.

They also had that pomade, that just-pressed
  white shirt, those syrupy phrasings,
that lush orchestration—those violin
  and horn sections—yet these were like
the candy shell for something else,
  something that had no name but you'd know it
when you tasted it because it would race
  through your veins and into your skull like a brush fire,
whatever it was, and the flames of Hell
  would leap up where your brain used to be,
and you'd like it and you'd know what Kant meant

when he said that the sublime is better
  than the merely beautiful because it hurts.
And I am not talking about carnal desire;
  I am talking about what cannot be talked about,
as, for example, in the dreamboat mise-en-scène
  Sam Cooke describes in "We're Having a Party."
The cokes are in the icebox, the popcorn's
  on the table, the guy and his girl
are dancing to the radio—you know it can't last.
  There's more to come, though you don't know what it is,
just as you can hear more in the slight roughness

of Sam Cooke's buttered-popcorn voice
  in the January 12, 1963 live session
at the Harlem Square Club in North Miami.

Just think, JFK was still alive then
and good-looking, too. He was just as handsome
   as Sam Cooke. He was just as ingenuous
   as the rest of us, thinking things would go on
   as they always had: touch football
in the front yard, a clean little war here and there,
   some side action in the old sex department
but nothing for anyone to get upset about,

and all the while the economy just keeps on
   inching forward. And then it's November 22,
and the limo swings slowly around the corner,
   and, rip, suddenly there's a big seam
right down the middle of history:
   everybody starts locking their doors
at night, trick-or-treaters don't go out
   without their parents, and at least
one clean little war grows into a dirty big one
   and then fragments into a dozen
dirty little ones that never seem to end.

A year later, Sam Cooke, wearing only a sports coat
   and a pair of shoes, is shot to death
by the manager of a three-dollar-a-night motel;
   more than 200,000 people view his body,
and at his funeral Ray Charles sings a song
   called "Angels Keep Watching Over Me." Sam Cooke
sang like an angel. Sam Cooke makes me think
of Herman Melville. Sometimes when I hear
Sam Cooke's voice I feel as though I'm "speeding up,"
   as Robert Lowell used to say when he started to go
into one of his manic phases,

and that's when I feel about soul music what
   James Dickey must have felt about poetry when he said
it was "just naturally the greatest goddamn thing
   that ever was in the whole universe." Sometimes
I go out in the morning, and it is raining so hard
   that the vines seem ready to reach up out of the earth

and pull me down and drown me. And on other days
 the sun is out, and I still have the taste of a great cup
of coffee in my mouth, and there's already a hint of fall
 in the air, and my team won the night before,
and Sam Cooke is still dead.

Complicity

> *On ne parle pas du corde*
> *dans la maison du pendu.*
>   —traditional French saying

A dog kills a chicken
on the farm where I am born,
and my mother ties the dead bird
to his collar. The dog looks sorry
for a day or two; the chicken,
rank and muddy, is taken away
and burned. And I, who feed
both dogs and chickens, wonder
if I will ever have to face the world
with my sins around my neck.

These days I have no dog,
and the only chickens I see
are in restaurants. I eat them
with potatoes and green peas,
and when the waiter whispers,
"Each of us has done something terrible,"
I ask him to please, be quiet
before the other customers hear:
one should not speak of rope
in the house of the hanged.

I Think I Am Going to Call My Wife Paraguay

I think I am going to call my wife Paraguay,
for she is truly bilingual,
even though she speaks no Guaraní
and, except for "cucaracha" and "taco,"
hardly any Spanish at all.
She has two zones, though,
one a forest luxuriant with orchids
and the smell of fruit trees,
where the Indians worship
the pure and formless Tupang,
who shines in the lightning
and roars in the thunder,
the other a dry plain,
a flat place with the soul of a mountain,
motionless and hard as a rock.
During the day the sun blazes
on the red dust of Paraguay
as dark-eyed, straight-backed women
walk home from the river
with bundles of laundry on their heads,
hoping to avoid trouble,
for the Paraguayans are always fighting;
young conscripts lolling in faded cotton uniforms
have no idea whether they will be summoned next
to overthrow the government or defend it.
My wife Paraguay and I
ourselves had to fight the War of the Triple Alliance,
although in our case
it wasn't Brazil, Uruguay, and Argentina
but Harry, Edward, and Maurice,
her former boyfriends. I won.
War does not silence Paraguay
or dismay her in any way,
for still her people shout on the football fields
and whisper declarations of love

on the darkened patios of the old colonial houses,
just as my wife Paraguay says that she loves me
as the parroquet and toucan fly over
and the perfume of the lime and orange tree
blow through the windows of our big house,
which I call South America
because it contains Paraguay
and is shaped like a sweet potato.

Baths

> *Nearly all the* Iliad *takes place far from hot baths. Nearly all of human life has always passed far from hot baths.*
> —Simone Weil

Baths are one more thing
to be separate from:
the steam,
the sweet slick of soap,
the unhurried attention
to nail and crevice,
the water rising,
the wet hair.
The senses sleep and wake—
something tolls you back,
a word like a bell,
and you go
to whatever calls you
from this tub
to the next.
Distance itself is a bath:
the mind walks over white tile,
past wooden benches
and narrow doors,
and keeps walking.

A. McA. Miller

Rowing

        we steered from the sun,
turned down on barrier
islands, veering so dark rose
from the water; it
spotted Father's khaki as
he dipped and feathered,
swung the oar-shafts down. "Time to
break," he said. He tipped
our boat with his weight, cooling
his hands in water.
"Anyway, it's time to bail."
I scooped a slosh of gray salt-
water overboard;
it trailed a small swirl backwards.
Westward, the Bay slid
wide fire to our boat.

        That August we'd caulked it: gray
seams sealed the flat white
floor. It dried for weeks, belly
up in the back yard;
boards had shrunk apart like Old
Dog's teeth. Then we'd grooved
the loose string paste in
tight, chisels scraping planks.
That caulking almost
held. A heavy sweat of water
seamed the starboard prow;
we'd quit, that August, early.

Isle of Flowers

     Now the boat drooled loose
water heavy as ice-tea
mugs had sweated in our hands.
We rode in a swill of seamed
white wood. He leaned, he
touched the water, overboard;
"Anyway, there's more
out there, than here," he said.
Our rowboat tipped out
far as his shoulders leaned, then
steadied; he balanced
the chipped green bench. "Dark's not so
bad. You just look out for light."

     Where headlights were
was home. As long as tourists,
drunks, and the late night
fishermen kept rolling towards
Shell Point, we'd find our
way. "If it rains," he said, "just
follow mangroves home."
The sun turned down: dark, salted
steamy. Sunset came
that way in forty-seven.
We'd caught one trout, two
blow-toads, one brown mad flounder.

     It glared up; two eyes
sparked from its left-hand face; its
teeth wide as your thumb
chewed air. I leaned, but
our boat didn't tilt. It bobbed
as he stroked the oars:
dip to pull, then feather back,
then dip. Its prow dipped
in a new slow glide. First the
left oar, then the right,
spread cool green swirls. Long water
boiled with color, all
the same, as if incoming

110

sea looked up through warm
Bay water. Oars pulled
down; as his leather shoes dug
suction from the boards,
we moved. I trailed my fingers
over the stern. Each
glowed and wavered. Brightness tracked
my fingers, leading
home. His blades pulled steady, greened,
then left their light; they
dipped the dark again.

Her Olds "Firenza"

       She'd swapped three rusted tons
of Chevy for that Lady's Car,
and gave the bandits ten grand more—
in the parlor of Hogan's Olds where posters
glowed with happy grey-haired women safe
behind their tilt-a-wheels, and automatic
windows. I really tried
to love that car.
It was her choice and treasure.
       So I fluffed the blue-fuzz carpets,
waxed its thin plastic leather,
buffed the clever fiberglass "bonnet,"
and polished that plastic chrome.
Still it lugged and halted.
       When the first stroke took her one good eye,
I became Chauffeur. No way, we couldn't
sell that car. It must become my favorite
even though her wheelchair wouldn't fit
its dinky trunk.
       And, lord, the Medical Miles
we logged—back and forth to ocular torture
("You'll see, Dear, I can't be blind") with Mother
jack-knifed in the front seat, and her walker
wedged under her chin.
       They jimmied her eyelids
up with clamps, and flashed more red lights
in the lens. Then Medicare ran out.
Driving home, her fingers clawed through vinyl.
Nu-Cote wouldn't seal it. That summer, heat split
hairlines down the fiberglass.
She couldn't see them, but her feet
balled up the blue-fuzz carpets
till I scraped them clean with Dad's straight razor.
       The windows jammed. She couldn't stand the summer
so I left them up, and flooded us with cold.
Then she couldn't stand the winter,

but its heater-coils kept leaking
on her slippers.
                  Come spring, the manifold
cracked open so its engine banged exhaust
and still we drove that Olds from Oculist
to Dentist, to Podiatrist and the savvy specialist
who readjusted her congested heart
with pills that flushed her urine down
the way I'd rod a radiator out.
Adult diapers wouldn't hold it.
                She never asked about the car.
Christmas morning, when she died,
I took a spin in my new Toyota,
and there, on Highway Forty-One,
I swear to god, was a junk-truck
crammed with cars, and one of them
was a blue and wrinkled Oldsmobile
smashed down and sideways like a box.

Obsession

for Miss Paam (Bên Cát, Vietnam)

Rain circled on your hooch. Late every night
Your legs, like new *Go Mat*, forked yellow brown.
If I plant you in the mud will you grow up?

Southeast winds had slithered off of Nam;
By chopper, R&R was one long hop.
If you try to dam the Mekong, then you drown.

Rice ponds were pooling over. On my lap
You rode like *Nipd* bobbing, tight as *Tram*;
If I plant you in the mud will you grow up?

In Georgia I'm a distant, different man.
My woman is a long-nose, white and slack.
If you try to dam the Mekong, then you drown.

You were slippery in the eye, but from the hip
You paced as straight as rain walks through the *Quan*;
If I plant you in the mud will you grow up?

Outside the hooch, rain fell forever down.
We paddled in our bodies like the rain.
If I plant you in the mud will you grow up?
If you try to dam the Mekong, then you drown.

Hooch, hut; *Go Mat*, yellowish brown wood ripsawed for construction work; *chopper*, helicopter; *R&R*, military leave for Rest & Recuperation; *Nipd*, mangrove with slender floating seeds; *Tram*, a dense wood, often flawed in the grain; *Quan*, a province or small state.

Enid Shomer

Global Aphasia

It's like a two-way street, the hospital speech
therapist explains, drawing lanes with arrows

and curves. Information swerves in through the ears;
replies arrive in the mouth. The brain is the driver.

"Okay okay okay," Mother answers without delay
when asked about the food, her health, this task.

This "automatic response," a kind of static, relieves
the silence she emotes like a high-frequency note

of distress. "Brush your...?" "Suitcase," she rushes to fill
in the blank, shaking her head as you would to free the ink

in a ballpoint pen. "Tie your...?" Mother's eyes roll.
"Suitcase?" she pleads. At the root of "perseveration," the name

for this odd repeating of words, is the word "persevere,"
that hopeful bird which sits on my chest with its head

snaked under a wing and its talons digging in as she shakes
more and more suitcases loose from her mind. One shines

on her finger, one barks like a dog. O singer with your one-word
song, you knew I was there but not for how long, so all

day you conjured up luggage, all day you lured my bags
from the thicket of thought and picked at the locks of my visit.

Sun and Moon in Mrs. Sussman's Tap Dancing Class

Mrs. Sussman is over fifty.
That is why her knees dimple
and her ankles slouch.
Her creamy thighs curdle under mesh tights
as she demonstrates a time-step.

Buck-and-wing and Hadassah
keep her busy. Once a Rockette,
she schools us in *stage presence.*
But even stars have to keep accounts
so she pins notes to our coats

if payment is late. I go home
saying ENID STILL OWES FOR FEB.
Mrs. Sussman helps make the costumes.
We spend one Saturday
up to our armpits in Rit Yellow #12

so that at the recital
we're convincing "rhythmic sunbeams."
I tap myself out
in my yellow muslin sheet
trying hard to think of

energy and *heat* when
what I really wanted was to be
the moon, that glacial beauty
which rose for a solo turn
after we had warmed the stage.

The moon is not important,
Mrs. Sussman said, explaining
why her daughter got the part.
The moon only reflects light
the sun makes. But I

wanted to be that moon
pulling a single spotlight
like a fur across the floor.
Lamé costume, jingle taps.
Glitter in my hair.

Even then in my patent leather
Mary Janes and primly folded socks
I wanted to be the moon
under which even city dogs howled
and men ventured out
for no good.

Cadillac

Imagine my squat, blue-eyed Russian
grandfather, a stogie in his fist, a Stetson

on his head, a silk suit precisely vented,
ordered from a rabbi with a sideline and friends

in Hong Kong. Imagine his voyage here alone
at thirteen, the sea like a pasture of fescue combed

by the wind and him below decks in that carousel
of piss and vomit. Imagine the babies crying, the charred smell

of food cooked in steerage, the dark knots
of men smoking and gambling. Did they hate

Jews, too? Imagine him on Ellis Island with his wild Slavic face
and the space between his shoulders that always

itched, puffing out his chest for the doctors.
One deep breath puts his name on the roster

Americanized—the *ik* chopped off of Magazinik
to make Magazine, a word he understands means a quick

book. He has no notion yet of luxury or charity, of leather
sofas or engraved plaques or dinners in honor

of. These will come after ice cream vending
and carpentry thin his voice and thicken his hands,

after he loses every cent in the Depression, and begins
his big ventures—Fort Stevens, Brandywine,

1000 Connecticut Avenue, that soaring granite address
that was like the White House for us,

a sparkling tower where he sat like a prince
thirty levels above the polished marble dance

floor of the lobby. O once more let him watch the phony
wrestlers on TV, his shoulders lurching with each throw.

I want to see him sop pleasure again from a bowl
with a heel of bread, dipping and slurping, his whole

face slick with broth and steam. And the deck
of nudie cards he kept hidden in the top right desk

drawer, redheads with tits like roses. And the slow
way he rolled up his "l"s on his tongue, as if savoring fish roe.

I remember how short he was behind the wheel of his prize—
they called them Jew canoes in those days—

how joyfully he packed us in on Sundays, plowing down the road,
letting the big car drift across the center line, like a parade.

Elegy And Rant For My Father

He grew up poor, believing only in luck.
His mother ran numbers; his father cut

hair. Hence the parimutuel tickets
embedded in the acrylic seat of his toilet,

the horses everywhere—nodding from chains on his chest,
petit-pointed jumping across his vest

buttons, wreathed in diamonds in a tiny
winner's circle that revolved on his pinky

ring. In old age he walked with his head hung
forward and down, as if a horseshoe were slung

around his neck. O heart like a fist! Nine
professional bouts as a bantamweight and then

his glass jaw shattered and all his promises broke.
When he was young and Miami was young, he worked

for the mob. Hair slicked back with sweet
pomades, he paid off deputies, placed bets.

O heart of pure gristle! He once paid a nickel
to sleep standing up in a Chicago flophouse, his satchel

strapped to his leg. He lacked ambition, waited
for things to break the way a fisherman waits

for the tide to turn and learns to love the quiet
spells between strikes, and learns to equate

his failures with his thrills. O heart like a serpent
knotted on itself! He was angry, he was ignorant

and nothing—not good suits or manicures
or flush nights or his wife's money—could secure

his signature on a check. Bad mortgage risk,
he was cursed and he cursed, his tongue a tusk

that gored you and left you bleeding in public
and still you covered for him. O heart like a hook!

He made you feel like a slut if your bra strap
showed, if you laughed too much or came home happy.

O heart like a cavern where you cried and kissed
at the darkness and mistook the echo of your own voice

for his! We buried him fourteen months later
than the doctor predicted. At the track that last year

with a wheelchair and oxygen tank: 85 pounds of hope
in stinking checkered pants and a baseball cap.

Adrenaline of the long shot, heart of an ox,
they said. At the grave, the lowering cord knocked

the Star of David off the coffin into the earth
and it was fitting because he was Jewish only by birth

and food and Yiddish joke. Still, they washed
his body devoutly and wrapped him head to toe in a wish—

a puffy white shroud like a cocoon where his last gamble,
a blue and white prayer shawl barely visible

through the gauze, lay like the colorful tips
of wings that would unfold in the next life.

Floating Islands

The afternoon we swam nude
in the Gulf, the sun struck against the sky
like a brand slowly cooling,
the waves twinging apart as if they'd
learned modesty, I wanted to touch
his hips tapering in the murky
depth, and pick up the white shells
of his feet. I wanted my breasts
to bob free of the sea's plunging
neckline and taste his salty hair
and push it back and kiss his forehead and kiss
underwater on the lips, our breath
rising like columns of mercury,
his arms drifting around me
like strands of kelp. I wanted the water
to slow down his desire, I'd said,
so he'd know how a woman feels it,
more like a feather drawn
across the flesh than a flame. For an hour
we floated, two shy camellias
in a shallow blue bowl. We talked
and treaded and kept our distance.
But that night in the shower he pressed
a leg between mine and asked could I
pee right then so he'd know the slow
warm sensation down a woman's thighs.

Rick Campbell

Hard Love

Close the bus terminal. Shut the train depot down.
Barricade all roads leading home.
Too many of us come back to this town.

We sit in these cheap beer bars and drown
the clean and shining places we have known.
Close the bus terminal. Shut the train depot down.

We follow roadmaps like dreams. We've been around.
The world couldn't keep us from straggling home.
Too many of us come back to this town.

We live here, where we were always bound.
Steel towns have ways of calling home their own.
Close the bus terminal. Shut the train depot down.

Protect us from ourselves. The siren's sound
lures our swingshift blood with its one-pitched tone.
Too many of us come back to this town.

We are veterans returning from the road. Surround
us with soot and ash, the coal barge's slow moan.
Close the bus terminal. Shut the train depot down.
Too many of us come back to this town.

Hanging Tobacco

for Daniel Scott

Blue gauze air, laces of light
bend through the barn. The peaked ceiling
smells like an old bar, walls soaked
in Camels. It hits your tongue
like your Grandfather's stained fingers.
He hugs your neck, his hand you taste
and keep.

But this is work. Love maybe,
the sweat and hurt, the one time
for the hell of it. Calves and thighs flicker.
Hands brown and sticky, face like a dustbowl
Okie's, this is a feeling
we'd be lying to claim we want for more than a day.
Lying to say it doesn't feel good here,
getting it done.

Seventh wagon. Leaves fat as Ohio catfish.
Tired of jerking lead-heavy sticks
from my ankles to the beams overhead,
I yell down to Daniel on the flatbed:
Sing. It's hot up here. Sing like we're having fun.

Chew my 'baccer, spit my juice
Gonna love my baby till it ain't no use
An' ho, ho baby, take a whiff on me.

I'm straddling the rafters singing
into the charred roof. The songs hang
in the thick air and curl around the barn.
Down below the song turns bawdy.
My hips remember a better ache, a better reason

to push for the ceiling. If there's a wrong time
to dream of making love, this is it.
Thirty feet up in a tobacco barn. No net.

They say you get high on your first smoke.
In the last six hours I've sucked down
every Pall Mall since Truman beat Dewey.
Her red river hair flows over my hands,
eyes blue as the late sky outside
the slatted vents of the barn.
This is a dangerous business.

Last spike hung. Climb down the wall
like a gray spider, stretch from beam
to beam to pull the muscles long again.
Whiskey cuts the stale air in our throats.
Back of the truck we're belting Leadbelly blues—
You take Sally an I'll take Sue—
down the red clay roads home.

Leaving Home, Pittsburgh, 1966

From the gray sky and the gray river,
we come in one day to the New World.
Though passage is no longer arduous and slow,
its displacement is sudden and complete.
The plane lifts into cold January
and the new year finds us becoming something
we don't understand. In high sun, sharp sky,
we stand on a bleached concrete runway
and wobble in the overwhelming light
to a small white terminal.
We are instant Floridians, squinting
as we turn and see nothing but sky
and thin palms rising from the flat land.
Our lives change in a hurry,
the way immigrants crossed
the sea, changed names and remembered
when they looked at photos,
at old letters, that their lives before
were lived at a different speed
in a different language.
The next morning we wake, forget
our way, our geography
and are scared again by the light,
the orange trees shining in the yard,
the talk of alligators in the canal.
Everywhere we see the strange world
we have to learn to live. Soon
our tongues are making long vowels, slowing,
warming to our task.

Ohio River Sunday

I liked to say
et cum spiritu tuo
and imagine
tutuos echoing as they
escaped the drab brick walls
of St. John's church, rising
like doves in the pictures,
like the Holy Spirit,
and then, realizing
they were free, taking off
up river, going North
where the sky was clean
and white barns dotted green fields.

I liked the tangible church,
the archeological smoothness of the cold,
rubbed pew. The way the palms
of Slovak workers darkened and shined
the wood as they shuffled to communion.
I liked to kneel in the shiny indentations.
A boy could wander along,
watching the rosary beads slide
through his grandmother's liver-spotted hands
until he was lost in his missal
and the strange-tongued prayers.

I was jarred back to my hard wood
when the lambs were swept on a tide
toward the altar to receive the host.
I sat exposed, a boy who'd missed confession.
I wanted to go to the rail like some glowing bird,
pluck the wafer and see if behind my closed eyes
whispered prayers rose toward the sooty windows,
joined the doves, and drifted off to God.

The Geography of Desire

If you insist on history
it was Cambridge, 1977. The door
of your flat closed and you disappeared
into the life you thought yours. I walked
streets caked with the winter's last snow.
Spring came that night, though there was little
reason to notice. Nothing to believe.

For years I made you every dark-haired woman
in the streets of Montreal, a bar
in St. Croix. I carried you with me
until now, the moment when our lives
break loose, like sailboats slipping
their moorings.

For years I have practiced stealing you.
Those nights when you dreamed
of flying over a land green with magnolia
and water oak, when you woke damp,
sea air on your neck, when,
for two days, every time you closed your eyes

you saw the Atlantic, I did that.
Those splitshot seconds when you turned
a corner, and everything danced, then settled,
you were living on the border.
I've honed desire beyond time and space

and bent geography into a New World.
This cartography of the heart
is stronger than any map that says Tucson,
any phonebook that says Calle Madrid.

Forget that other life.
It's just a hole between the last time I saw you
and now, this life, our life.

Christy Sheffield Sanford

Traveling through Ports that Begin with "M"

Mobile
1930
(Shrimp)

Jack scrubs the smell of hemp and tar from his hands and weaves his way along the waterfront. He's picking up Pearl. She doesn't want to go. Sure, they were childhood sweethearts, but now she's a platinum blond selling her body to merchant marines and shrimpers. Finally, he visits "Seven Sister," the conjure woman in Hogansville. She tells him to swab sweat from his right armpit, mix it with cologne, and dab it on the desired lady. He has to hold Pearl down to do that. Later she says, "It was your desperation, not spells, that won me."

Maracaibo
1935
(Snapper)

Sweat rolls down Jack's face as he climbs over a derrick. It's 82° and almost time for siesta. Schools of yellow-tail snapper leave the ocean to dart in and around the lake. Mosquitos thrive in spite of the fish. At first, Jack's body is strong. Then malaria flattens him. Beside a lone orange hibiscus, Pearl sets a chair. She clips the hair of oil riggers and with her intimate touch she earns enough to book passage on a coffee boat to Marseilles. Her uncle Leon de Lesseps has offered his aid once they land.

Marseilles
1940
(Octopus)

In a hospital near the quai, Jack tosses with an afternoon fever. A storm rumbles through the harbor. Pearl's bedroom chandelier sways and tinkles in the wind. In a dream she watches the light turn into an octopus. Tentacles unfurl and squeeze her. She wakes in Leon's sleep-laden embrace. "Men's sex organs are so much alike," she muses. Something she'd forgotten. She pats his haunch, slips on her robe and walks into the garden to plant basil and mint for Jack's tea. He's almost well. Pearl considers joining the French Resistance.

Manila
1945
(Shark)

Jack enters the city by crashing through the wall in a U.S. tank. He stays to help Filipinos clean up the rubble. Pearl didn't think she could have children, but here she is suckling a war baby. With Jacqueline on her hip she works for the Red Cross — bathing and barbering the wounded. One day on the way home, she swoons against a shop. The facade crumbles. She and Jacqueline barely escape. Meanwhile Jack lends a hand to a guy hoisting a catch and loses three fingers to a requiem shark.

Mazatlan
1950
(Sailfish)

Glazed sailfish stud the wall of the yacht club. Jack finishes a Cuba Libre and climbs aboard his sleek cruiser. A "billfishing" expert, he's taking out a couple of rich Texans for a rodeo. Jack tugs at his cap's bill with its scrambled eggs and secures a shirt-button over his tan stomach, protruding above bermudas. Nearby in his backyard, Jackie, now five, says, "Get back in there!" as she pokes at a scorpion in a jar. In the house Pearl stirs iced tea for Jack's dinner. She adds a sprig of mint and bruises the leaves lightly against the rim of the glass.

Hurricane! Alex!

At Cape Verde on the African west coast, storms David and then Frederic were spawned. When they became organized, with 74 mph winds, they graduated to hurricane status.

The glass pops out of the bedroom window of my stilt house on Mobile Bay. I look out, see Alex struggling to reach his Mercedes 450SL.

"Hurricane" derives from Maya and Carib Indian words for devil, evil spirit, storm god. Severe storms create a lot of noise; Frederic barrels into Mobile Bay wailing like a banshee.

Alex, I yell. A galvanized tin roof like a gigantic flying razor blade slices through the right front window of his car.

Nine out of ten deaths in hurricanes occur from drowning in storm tides or surges of water that sweep ashore with driving winds.

Alex, I scream, as a 13-foot wall of water heads straight toward him. I rush down the back steps.

David batters the Caribbean with torrential rains and winds gusting to 175 mph. And Frederic, a monster unable to control his direction, strengthens in David's wake.

The tide tows Alex under. He lies face down in a shallow pool 50 feet away. Palm fronds arch and rattle over my head.

In Dominica, the air whips into a green froth of mud, water and coconuts; and in Mobile, uprooted oaks, stoplights and campers bounce across the streets.

You mustn't die, not now. I fight the wind, dodge flying objects. Finally bending over him, I check his pulse, listen for breathing.

A hurricane, like a hearth fire, requires air to flow from the bottom, to spiral up the chimney (the eye), and spill over the top.

He's drowning. I pull off his gold signet ring. Alex, you bastard, don't die. I climb on his back and push hard with deep rhythmic motions.

During the storm's confusion, looting occurs in Mobile. And in Dominica, thieves steal food, furniture, clothes, cars, even relief shipments.

Alex coughs, spits up and begins to breathe. He shakes his head — the head I've loved and hated for two years. My dress, wet gauzy cotton, sticks to my body like the fabric on a Greek statue.

August/September hurricanes typically survive only two weeks. Once over land, deprived of ocean warmth and moisture, they rapidly subside.

Now I know what I must do. I take a gob of my skirt, stuff it in Alex's mouth. I put both my hands over his nose and press. His eyes open — mine close. His arms flail, then his muscles slacken.

In Dominica, David kills 56 and destroys most of the banana crop. David rates 4 on the 1-5 Saffir-Simpson scale, with 5 being catastrophic. Frederic kills only five but makes a shambles of Mobile.

Women in ports all over the world cheer. I turn to go. Alex grabs my foot. Sara, he says.

Hurricanes deliver rain to barren regions and disseminate the extreme heat that accumulates in the tropics.

The only way to escape a guy like that is to move inland.

Barbara Hamby

The Language of Bees

The language of bees contains 76 distinct words for stinging,
    distinguishes between a prick, puncture, and mortal wound,
        elaborates on cause and effect as in a sting
            made to retaliate, irritate, insinuate, infuriate, incite,
            rebuke, annoy, nudge, anger, poison, harangue.
The language of bees has 39 words for queen—regina apiana,
    empress of the hive, czarina of nectar, maharani of the
        ovum, sultana of stupor, principessa of dark desire.
The language of bees includes 22 words for sunshine,
Two for rain—big water and small water, so that a man urinating
        on an azalea bush in the full fuchsia of April has the
        linguistic effect of a light shower in September.
For man, two words—roughly translated—"hands" and "feet,"
        the first with the imperialistic connotation of beekeeper,
        the second with the delicious resonance of bareness.
All colors are variations on yellow, from the exquisite
        sixteen-syllable word meaning "diaphanous golden fall,"
        to the dirty ochre of the bitter pollen
        stored in the honeycomb and used by bees for food.

The language of bees is a language of war. For what is peace
        without strife but the boredom of enervating day-after-day,
        obese with sweetness, truculent with ennui?
Attack is delightful to bees, who have hundreds of verbs
        embracing strategy, aim, location, velocity:
        swift, downward swoop to stun an antagonist,
        brazen, kamikaze strike for no gain but momentum.
Yet stealth is essential to bees, for they live to consternate
        their enemies, flying up pant legs, hovering in grass.

No insect is more secretive than the bee, for they have two
        thousand words describing the penetralia of the hive:
        octagonal golden chamber of unbearable moistness,
        opaque tabernacle of nectar,
        sugarplum of polygonal waxy walls.

The language of bees is a language of aeronautics,
        for they have wings—transparent, insubstantial, black-
        veined like the fall of an exotic iris.
For they are tiny dirigibles, aviators of orchard and field.
For they have ambition, cunning, and are able to take direct aim.
For they know how to leave the ground, to drift, hover, swarm,
        sail over the tops of trees.

The language of bees is a musical dialect, a full, humming
        congregation of hallelujahs and amens,
        at night blue and disconsolate,
        in the morning bright and bedewed.

The language of bees contains lavish adjectives
        praising the lilting fertility of their queen:
        fat, red-bottomed progenitor of millions,
        luscious organizer of coitus,
        gelatinous distributor of love.
The language of bees is in the jumble of leaves before rain,
        in the quiet night rustle of small animals,
        for it is eloquent and vulgar in the same mouth,
        and though its wound is sweet it can be distressing,
        as if words could not hurt or be meant to sting.

St. Anthony of the Floating Larynx

We take a train to Padua to see the Giottos, lapis and gold,
and the mostly-destroyed Mantegna frescoes of the life

of St. James, blown to bits by a wayward American bomb,
patched together like a puzzle now, but with most of the pieces
   missing.

My friend is on a pilgrimage to the Cathedral of St. Anthony
of Padua, patron saint of harvest, lovers, sick animals,

and lost objects, *oggetti* in Italian, and this church
is quite an *Oggetto* itself, with a capital "O,"

and I have seen my share of shrines in the last three months.
Immediately I recognize that this is no ordinary repository

of frescoes, plastic statuary, and other divine bric-a-brac.
It is a hive of religiosity, alive with bizarre reliquaries;

in fact we stand in line to see St. Anthony's larynx, yes indeed,
his voice box, suspended in a gelatinous scarlet liquid,

a cartilaginous snake of animal matter, from which my husband
(educated by Jesuits) turns, white as a piece of typing paper.

This is the Italy I dreamed of, saints, snakes, gypsies,
cutthroats in a baroque tutu of religion and sin.

The venality of it all is like eating cake for breakfast,
though it's obvious that not much cake eating is going on

in the Cathedral of St. Anthony but rather atonement for cake
eating, for three quarters of the multitude in the church

are on their knees, reminding me of a Billy Graham Crusade
I attended as a twelve-year-old when the great man himself said,

"Fall down on your knees and pray for God's forgiveness."
It's an interesting concept, forgiveness, and one, I must say,

that appeals to the throng in Padua, or are they praying
for miracles? In a sense forgiveness is a miracle, or at least

for someone like me who finds pardon difficult and unfulfilling,
or as my friend Mary Ann Wolf used to say, "What good's a grudge

if you can't hold it?" What would St. Anthony have to say about
mercy? I wonder as I queue up with my friend at the saint's tomb.

She wants a husband and I want back the bag that Alitalia lost
three months ago in Rome. As I raise my arm to place my palm on

the wall of the tomb, a four-by-four grandmother dressed in
black cuts in front of me and knocks my arm out of the way.

Her problem is probably a lot more pressing than a suitcase
of dresses, which, by the way, St. Anthony delivers to me

a month later in the Miami airport. My friend is still single,
although her old boyfriend called and told her she was

the love of his life, not exactly her dream come true
but in the true-love ballpark. Maybe the saints do better

with material requests. A green silk dress has got to be easier
to deliver than a boyfriend with a job and a working personality.

Metaphysics is so tiring, which is what St. Anthony would
probably say if he could, lying in that tomb, sans larynx, teeth,

and assorted other body parts. Day after day, we line up with our
problems, raise our troubled palms. "Maria? No, my friend, she's

wrong for you. It won't last more than a year." And the poor guy
goes off, thinking, That Maria, I could really be happy with her.

The Ovary Tattoo

Etched on my abdomen like a botanical illustration
is the reproductive paraphernalia of a flower

or *facsimile animalis*, the oviduct named for
Gabriello Fallopio, Italian anatomist,

no artist but a careful researcher, his vellum
untouched by the meandering entrails on the table,

untidy detritus of tissue and blood, a reminder that,
above all, God is Albrecht Dürer, an expert draftsman,

peculiar in his tastes, untidy but organized, peripatetic,
not particularly ecstatic in the connubial state and bent

on a sort of subtle revenge, for bare form tells all,
the apparatus itself like antlers or the antennae

of some marvelous insect, a bee, *apis mirabilis*,
yet on its side becomes a spilled cup or pincers

and darker still when capsized, an anchor,
ponderous iron, pulling hull, mast, sail, sailors

into the unfathomable bowels of primal craving. Some say
love is a cave, unlit and mysterious, or do they say

it's a long corridor in a lavish French château
lined with mirrors, icy laughter caught on the dripping

crystals of chandeliers? I forget. Perhaps it's both,
a declivity and *une galerie des glaces*, goldleaf nymphs

bearing platters of light into musty caverns beneath
the castle, the sheen of their skin in candlelight

belying the bastinado of blood, evil and completely
seductive, Scheherazade on a cellular level, because

if there is one thing about love that I will never
understand, it's how pale it is, unaccustomed to daylight,

yet how it seems to live in the mad drumming of the blood
and then can sit in the chest like a high-toned cleric who, upon

closing his lesson book, crawls along the intestinal tract
like a transvestite demagogue, preaching to the E. coli

and the mutating cells, "Replicate, breed, multiply, procreate,
propagate, proliferate, make more babies for God,"

until every square inch of ground is awash in humanity,
the mad pulse of a trillion aortas, the tick, throb,

stroke, thump, pant of blood rising like a deep jungle moan:
we are hungry, we are angry, we are helpless, we are here.

Judith Berke

Poem Beginning in the Bed of My Mother and Father

If I am the wedge
I am also the pillow
between them, there
in the crack where the beds

come together. Perhaps
even then I think
I can join them
like the piece of flesh

between Siamese twins.
Perhaps when I'm not there
he is holding her
from in back, like the two

waves, the dark and light
of a Chinese symbol.
Or maybe they're
back to back

as helpless as any
instruments
of torture—
but right now the sun

comes in, leafy and sweet
as it is in winter, in the morning.
It is perfectly safe
to look into

the two faces—
and no, I am not them—
the "no" and the "I" tell me,
and yet I am sinking into them

like butter.
Disappearing into
the softness between them.
Maybe that's what we look for

our whole lives: the absolute
separateness,
at the very moment
we disappear into each other.

The Strangler Fig

The cabbage palm was very much alive.
Some of its leaves were hay-like, droopy,
but the shiny green leaves of the fig tree
growing among them, around them, gave it a brilliance.

You could still see the one straight
very tall trunk
of the palm and around it the roots
of the other, like some sort of horrible love.

It was the birds
that brought the seeds of the fig tree
to the shy, folded-up leaves of the palm
but there was no use hating the birds.

Might as well hate the ground
which does not allow
the other to grow up very well
so naturally it has to grow downward.

Might as well hate the cabbage palm
itself. For not having thorns,
and for the criss-cross pattern of old leaf
bases around it, which make it

such a good place to grow down into.
Might as well hate the wasps
for not having pollinated
the fig tree. Though who knows

if this kind has any figs at all.
We were only there for the shade
that day; did not want
anything else from it.

Madre Del Olvido

after the drawing by Lucia Maya

Because she does not weep with her eyes
   her whole body
is weeping. Her head so heavy it's pulling
her down, bending her at the waist
   as if she were bowing.
More like a broken tree than a woman.

And yet she is young. A moment ago
she was dancing in her bare feet
in the grass. Her hair weeping
   even as she danced,
her hair waving like water.

"I am never going to die,"
she thought, but her head began to ache;
she couldn't hold it up—
no more than a willow
can hold up its leaves.

The next moment she was like this:
as if being pulled to the earth
head first. But not really seeing
   the earth.
Her palms pressed to her chest
in this gesture.

Triple Toe Loop

Never mind the skater who does the jump
as if she'd been a top in a previous incarnation.
Watch the one who falls

and picks herself up, and falls
and picks herself up again.
How in the slow part

she holds her hands out with the palms up
as if to say, This is the best I can do
at this moment. A fire-

bird yes, but the story
she's skating is anyone's story. Look
the bird has no wings at all. See what long

arms the bird has. Spinning
up there. Holding her arms
in front of her, the way I did

when the man who loved me was shocked to see
me actually naked—
that is without any *kind* of perfection—

and I wished for one of those dreams
where you can fly—against
the heaviness of the earth.

Against the earth, and in love with it.

We Know Now

We know now the awful snarl
on the face of Gargantua
was a burn, a wound.
The truth was in his slumped shoulders,

the sad inward gaze that is
a gorilla. And yet
we didn't know, knew nothing,

as the moment in '45
when the cruel, inhuman
Japanese soldiers
stepped out of the posters
and bowed so gracefully before us.

How can we go on? How do we stand it?
The dinosaurs lie down
so quietly, so suddenly,
and up come the tiniest lizards.

And we? Later? Do we just
slide quietly under?
Do I choose you? As delicate
as a Himalayan monk?

Who will tell us? The moon,
not even alive, and pulls so terribly on our bodies,

the cells, the genes below that
singing only
blue eyes, blue eyes, blue eyes...

Silvia Curbelo

Photograph of My Parents

I like the way they look together
and how simply her smile floats towards him
out of the dim afterglow

of some memory, his hand
cupped deliberately
around the small flame

of a match. In this light
nothing begins or ends
and the camera's pale eye

is a question that answers itself
in the asking. *Are you there?*
And they are. Behind them

the wind tears down and blows
apart, angel of nonchalance.
The world belongs to the world.

For years he smoked down to the filters
sorting out the pieces of his life
with the insomniac's penchant

for detail. In the heart's
heavy forest, the tree of self-denial,
the bough, the single leaf

like the blade of a word held back
for a long time. The moment
she leans towards him the room

will become part of the story.
The light is still as a pond.
My mother's blue scarf

is the only wave.

Drinking Song

after Schumann

In every half-filled glass a river
begging to be named, rain on a leaf,
a snowdrift. What we long for

precedes us. What we've lost
trails behind, casting
a long shadow. Tonight

the music's sad, one man's
outrageous loneliness detonated
into arpeggios of relief. The way

someone once cupped someone's
face in their hands, and the world
that comes after. Everything

can be pared down to gravity
or need. If the soul soars with longing
the heart plunges headfirst

into what's left, believing
there's a pure want
to fall through. What we drink to

in the end is loss, the space
around it, the opposite
of thirst, its shadow.

Tonight I Can Almost Hear the Singing

There is a music to this sadness.
In a room somewhere two people dance.
I do not mean to say desire is everything.
A cup half empty is simply half a cup.
How many times have we been there and not there?
I have seen waitresses slip a night's
worth of tips into the jukebox, their eyes
saying *yes* to nothing in particular.
Desire is not the point.
Tonight your name is a small thing
falling through sadness. We wake alone
in houses of sticks, of straw, of wind.
How long have we stood at the end of the pier
watching that water going?
In the distance the lights curve along
Tampa Bay, a wishbone ready to snap
and the night riding on that half promise,
a half moon to light the whole damned sky.
This is the way things are with us.
Sometimes we love almost enough.
We say *I can do this, I can do
more than this* and faith feeds
on its own version of the facts.
In the end the heart turns on itself
like hunger to a spoon.
We make a wish in a vanishing landscape.
Sadness is one more reference point
like music in the distance.
Two people rise from a kitchen table
as if to dance. What do they know
about love?

Last Call

I know the man who eavesdrops
at the bar means no harm,
that he washes his hands of what is said,

that if his coffee grows cold
it isn't loneliness.

I know it isn't fear that leads
a beast to water, that sleep
comes down upon the blessed,

that when a good man drinks
the child inside him begins to close his eyes.

I know when the actress lifts her glass
that the movie continues, a role
she has slipped on like a raincoat
but there's no rain,

that in an avenue of trees and
perfect lawns the world is infinite.
The doorman leaning on somebody's
Cadillac loses track of time, his eyes fixed
on the beautiful map of anywhere.

And I know in small towns all over America
the jukeboxes are rigged,
that somewhere a man takes the wrong
woman in his arms and on a dance floor
a love song falls gently to its knees.

And I know the dark begins and ends
in a place we know by heart,
that sleep runs like a river through it,
and sooner or later we are all baptized.

By now the last insomniacs
are gathering their car keys and
drifting home to their books
and the all-night religious channel

and a voice climbs down an open window
across the dark tenements of salvation softly,
across the silent tract houses,

down among the sleepwalkers; their dreaming
eyes are shut.

Bedtime Stories

after Marc Chagall

Say it isn't real.
Say this violin is not a window.
The rose opening up from its shadowy heart
conceals its stupid thorn
like a child before his first mirror.
But a painting is not a mirror.
The colors are not real.
The flowers swaying in the hushed light
tell us a different story
and the child drifting through a landscape
of trees and numbers cannot hear it.

The trees are the one constant,
always touching the earth
but reaching for something else.
The violin itself is not color
but lightness. The music
rising beyond the highest
branches imitates flight,
sleep, a kind of floating.
This happens long before the idea
of falling enters the picture.
We attempt to grow graceful and weightless.
We leave our shoes behind.

This is the pure air of a painting
like a child before an open window
waiting for someone to begin
the next story, to bring him
his nightly drink of water
or lay beside him on the little bed.
The bed can be a mirror,
but not as real,
not at all like a painting

or a rose. His head resting
on the pillow is so sweet.
It could never be a tree,
it grows inward, rootless,
floating towards sleep.

Already we know this story
is not real, the colors
are too vague. The child
closes his eyes and imagines
the rest of his life
like a dream about falling
from a great height.
But this is early on,
before sleeplessness, before
he comes to terms with the idea
of gravity and the window
shuts completely in his dreams.
He will lose track of the story.
He will stare at the ceiling.
He will learn to count sheep.
This is a prelude to something else,
something that comes much later,
not sleep, but a kind of falling
through himself in layers,
a sheaf of numbers
adding up to the one belief,
a feeling he can count on,
the pure mathematics of desire.

It happens slowly. He begins to see
himself in multiples of two,
of four, the world unfolding
in a graceful symmetry, two lips,
two breasts, then his own longing
multiplying, becoming
a mirror to the girl
who is beautiful, who lies
in his two arms, who is
like a painting or a rose

Isle of Flowers

or music going on somewhere else.

This happens earlier,
before he learns to think in multiples
of three, before coming face
to face with his two hearts,
the other one that grows
much later, that thorn
leading up to the first kiss,
the first betrayal, the other woman
concealed behind a smokescreen
of desire. These too are dreams
about falling. He falls out of step,
falls short, falls for a woman
the way a child falls asleep
before the story ends.

He has now entered a world beyond
all his calculations. He begins
to count backwards to the first
color, the first sleep, the first
music playing. That happens earlier,
much earlier, before he learns to count
on this completely: Love ends,
stories go on untold
for years, the colors fade
into the background, vanish beneath
the body's clumsy light.

But this is not a painting
he can live with. The trees are thick
and ugly. His own face floats
out of any mirror
like the soul out on a limb,
no longer a child facing an open window
but a man having learned
the weight of dreams.

The Lake Has Swallowed the Whole Sky

Some dreams are like glass
or a light beneath the surface of the water.

A girl weeps in a garden.
A woman turns her head and that is all.

We wake up a hundred times and
don't know where we are. Asleep

at the wheel. Saved by
the luck of angels.

Everyone touching his lips
to something larger, the watermark

of some great sorrow. Everyone
giving himself away. The way

the rose gives up its stem and
floats completely, without history.

In the end every road leads
to water. What is left of a garden

is the dream, an alphabet of longing.
The shadow of the girl. Perfume.

Steve Kronen

The World Before Them

Actually, it was sweet and heavy with juice
and we passed it back and forth, a river
of nectar running down her chin and mine
until we were full and our faces shone
and could not tell receiver from giver.
I loved its weight in my hand, bruised
just a little from having fallen
from those high, green limbs. And we took its seed
and planted more when we left that place
so we'd always be sure to have its taste
upon our tongues. That was her idea, freed
us from worrying about the future. And all in
all, we didn't. We ate them to the core.
It's as though we'd been provided for.

In the Hangar of Brisbee, Oklahoma, 1933

Sleepy, my father liked to lie on its floor and stare
through the August heat at the quivering air gathered above

as if it were the dome of heaven and he lay
at the top of the beneficent world dreaming of flight

—all of them together once more—Mom, Pop, and son
packed like bonbons into their seats, white scarves

flapping like birthday ribbons. How he'd pray, he told me,
that the pilot would take them up where the thin wind

makes the eyes tear and carry them all across the farm
where his parents were raised—two bucktoothed cousins

hauling milk between the barn and wagon. And there
they'd see the farmhouse and the chalky soil, sky rippling

like the Northern Lights over the quilt that unraveled
beyond the grey roofs of Brisbee and Clover City.

How they'd marvel at themselves, a family in flight,
and at their shadow, no larger it seemed, than the decimal
   point

that brought the loan officer to their porch, than the pupil
still swimming in his milky eye.

The Awful Balance

When my grandfather was dying,
my mother would read to him his favorite passage:
Only this evening I saw again low in the sky
The evening star, at the beginning of winter, the star
That in spring will crown every western horizon,
Again...
And since his memory was like an empty shelf
she read the same piece each day
and he took delight in it over and over.
And just as a sailor turns a stone in his mouth
to slake his thirst,
my grandfather turned the words
until they slid from the morphined pillow of his brain.

Once the stars had risen
she'd place him by the bay windows
where his body filled with salt air.
And though too cold, it no longer mattered,
its comfort greater than its threat, the breeze
pressing itself upon him as easily as sleep a child,
and his eyes, refusing no world,
told us he was still half here
and so half elsewhere.

Vermeer also placed those he loved most
by open windows, allowing the light from without
to illuminate his subjects' faces
nearly as much as by their own quiet domesticity.
How many times did that woman read that letter
repeating those phrases that made her most happy
until remembering a meal needed preparing
or water fetching
she folded the letter and placed it in her blouse
thinking no further of it but allowing
its presence about her moving body
to make each chore simple and pleasurable?

The awful balance, Ellie, fearing
that which we love most will be taken from us
and never return. I imagine now that he has returned
growing large inside your belly. When I kiss your eyes
and you say my name over and over
we are on a raft,
the perfect shift of weight
keeping us afloat.
Your eyes the blue of her blouse, the color of the sailor's sky.

Isle of Flowers

Mayflies

> *A given distance can be halved ad infinitum.*
> —Zeno's dichotomy

They use assiduously their given time,
Some texts say twenty-four hours,
Others ten or twelve. In World War I
When flying was novel enough
That bombs were dropped by the pilot's own hand,
My grandfather, watching from above,
Tried to follow their graceless descent
Tracing the long golden section described
Till they flashed, white and silent,
The way serotonin does
On some hillside of the brain.
Later at the university, when he taught
How the wide array of the animal kingdom
Flew, crawled, or swam themselves
Toward the unseen glory
That willed their locomotion,
He spoke of the mayfly, how its heart
Was proportionately the same size
As the human's and beat
In such furious synch with the blurred wings
It could, were it large enough, induce seizure
In an epileptic. Such timing, he explained,
Allowed a machine gun to be mounted
On the nose of a biplane
And never shoot its own propellers.
The mayfly, if extrapolated to human terms,
Would live to be eighty.

It is the first cool night of autumn, 1964.
My grandfather tells me
There is less space between the two stars
That float above us like shy teenagers
Than between any two electrons

Whirling within the heart.
This, I think, is how love works—
Were I to ride light, like some angelic
And fevered horse, the great arc of space
Like the shell of the tortoise that holds the world,
Would forever bring me back here to myself.
And I think I understand—how a circuit once completed
Has no beginning nor end and we, like Zeno's runner,
Live forever between here and there, between the lubb and the dubb
Of the beating heart, arising once and always,
Like Jesus, incorruptible, from the cave. And all around us
The air is hushed but for two crickets
Calling back and forth, tiny and splendid,
Across the chilling night.

Gail Shepherd

The Owl

Three times she swooped low without
moving anything she touched;
the air she flew through undisturbed
fit her body like a glove.

The sun set early, hills dissolved;
flake by flake the barns sloughed off
the sheen of place, their painted reds
sifting into leaves and earth.

She arrowed the world uncompromised.
No feather of her patterned wing
traced her patterns back to us.
We watched our forms unraveling:

dying light had mined with blues
the edges we had cultivated.
Our shadows rearranged themselves
along the field's articulations

and pressed the grasses sadly down
as if they'd turned our solid freight
to water in their shifting walls:
a liquid laced with scent of ash

drifting from our neighbor's house.
The owl repeated her only question;
darkness canceled out the answer.
Knot of contact, thread of release,

they say that if you cut owl's heart
and set it on your lover's breast,
she'll tell her secrets while she sleeps.

First Questions

Love, the cynics have it, comes
dressed as a blind man. And the virgin lifts her lantern

to his silvered eyes, or catches her fashionable
reflection doubled on dark lenses, and thinks

of herself, suddenly, as less precious, less remote,
delivered into those hands

so finely attuned to pleasure,
whispering nonsense into an ear as sensitive to nuance

as the ear of a stag, as the ear of a shell.
The story has various endings—

folly and sin, self-deception and servitude...
I prefer to imagine love as patiently Socratic,

not as a figure at all
but a series of questions

devolving with the pleasant click of celluloid
reengaging its sprockets, say, at the close of a film.

Will I love you forever? Are you willing to go?
What largesse we demand then,

while the lights of boats flicker yes, no, yes
with just the right balance and introspection

necessary to those who make a living adrift.
The questions difficult to ask, the answers simple.

Girls at Confirmation

They are scraps of lace, a dressmaker's ribbon
unspooled, despoiled. From where the congregation stands
they're grained with dust and distance. That first communion,
its discomfiting clichés: demure hands,

the rustle of best dresses, a flurry as angel-moths
flutter up the aisle toward a myth
of heavenly incandescence, each pretty mouth
open for the tang of flesh and blood. As if

suffering could be traded with such innocence!
Seen from above, through God's fish-eye lens:
the girls in marriage whites, their parents
a blur of benevolence under the granite saint's

gray-blue regard, his oriental smile on the verge
of sensuality. Dome-light rests its lance
gently on the priest's shoulder. And hands
press host to tongue, hands urge

them back into the sun again. Already, in a borrowed car,
and out all afternoon, perhaps on Lovers' Hill,
they sit remotely, overlooking the stagger
of houses and spires, feeling dreamy, restless, evil.

Southern Weddings

1.
    Tents on a crab-pocked lawn are
  all potential; like furled parasols,
they look, from a third floor attic's viewpoint—for
        the bride is closeted there
on the bride's prerogative to stall
          indefinitely—
a measure of the way she'll soon unfold her
          white dress, unfold herself

    from the white dress, later on;
  and she imagines her naked feet,
strong, defensive, slipping off the satin
        shoes impetuously, then
the solemn seed pearls unclasped. If light
          always falls benign
on such mornings, then why does the black hound sit,
          like an omen of grief,

        beside the folded tents?
It's the way he seems to juxtapose
her human world with animal discontents
        annoys her: she has the sense
that life is sporadically composed
          by such negligence,
as once spilled ink had blotted her eloquent
          letter of refusal

        to the young man now waiting
on the lawn beside furled parasols,
who bends abstractedly to touch the panting
        dog, a gesture betraying,
just briefly, no tenderness at all
          but a charity,
like that with which, tonight, she'll let the white dress fall
          around her naked feet.

2.
        When the head of Orpheus
washed up on the red coast at Lesbos,
mouth plugged with seaweed, eyes permanently fogged
            to any beauty
save the harsh, interior moonscape of one
        relation, they called it an

        oracle: salt-preserved brains
working the future's capital gains
like a series of black notes on a white score.
            Those who listened heard
their lovers lamenting. Tonight a wildfire
        burns in the worthless scrub, scours

        brush down to embers the wind
disperses next day as finer sand
to clot the delphiniums spiking the yard,
            a bridal bouquet
threaded with cracks, like inherited china.
        How the spider skims down a

        silk lately appended to
the framed photograph taken of you
and nets the warm hearth with what broom will plunder
            with tomorrow's ash
depends on her health, forces of gravity,
        an inbred tenacity.

Peter Hargitai

Cats

are sudden.
Fiercer than jungle smelling,
an oil of brilliant colours,
they're so suddenly large.
Something with the eyes,
hair bristling several layers of mad.
I don't care for paintings of cats
eating the spine like flowers.
I had a little tiger of childhood,
a bed-warmer son of a bitch
that turned
as I knew it would.
And there's something
about turning.
It's black with streaks
of silver moving
through the air
like darts move.
For some time now I have avoided them
because they are so
classical.
After baby chicks have moved
into one's head cats come
near. Even in portraits.
I don't know—
something happens to kittens
and I associate violence with their
lovemaking. As the sudden-of-a-wave
they arch
and there is much to this sort of arching.
The same black and silver without warning

arches. I've seen it in oceans—
cowering in the corners of kitchens, crazy
to have a fondness for milk
and the smell of liver.
Something erotic about their black rubber tails
underneath the fur, the way they're almost male.

The Art of Taxidermy

Look for a blackbird flitting on the wire
thinking it to be a branch. Its coat, almost
blue, will glint a black angel toward heaven
before sparks singe the metallic beak
and breathe from it an animal smell.
It is to die, this means, despite the shining.

Take the worm from the mouth
and lop off the starry comb,
tossing the innards
to a whiskered cat. Inflate
with air until the bird is full
and clouds sail by. Cool. Spread
fine-needle frost to the wings.

Air cannot flush skin
no matter how much it is made to swallow.
Wait until the heart is still
or not there at all—

Then stuff it with the stars of night
known also as the stuff of dreams,
with care not to stretch the arsenic
skin. And when the green and marble eyes,
cooler than glass, light up the self-
illuminating body, it is time,
when the eyes flicker into glowworm,
it is time to serve the body.

Seeds

Nagymama,
you think my blood
lighter than it should be.
I have not enough reverence
for the texture of brown earth,
not the right kind of love
for its deep darkness. My hands
give me away without callouses. Only thoughts

in my head: one is a pied brooder, black and white.
It shivers a moment and gives off a smell.
I look down the throat of the furnace,
a few charred pieces of paper or feathers,
something dry floats
out of its mouth. It is August. I want to play soccer,
I want to run.
Your house smells like wheat, millet, poppyseed, lentils.
I saw a tail of a mouse squirm right in. I think
there are more of them. I am not happy diving into
a heap of seeds headlong like into water
like you thought
I would. What if there's something hidden?
What if I dive in, lose my breath,
and never come back.
If I should sink into that awful sea of seeds piled high
to the ceiling, you would never know how I gave my life.
The roof is a sieve. I breathe seeds. More of them than
even air. I see nothing else, I think, seeds upon seeds
upon seeds pour from the apron of the sky.

Mother's Visit No. 29

I think I will allow myself to get caught.

And not bother to vacuum the pool:
there are roaches on the bottom
I would like you to see.
Neither is the floor swept
nor the windows washed.
There are hairs on the couch,
I think a dog's.

Something smells in here

like raw fish.
Or black hair that is wet,
matted, and close to the skin.

But do come in. Do come in.

It is Easter of course.

I am waiting with the perfect gift:
a tiny spool of thread, a thimble, a needle
all in one egg.
Stuffed into an egg, a white plastic egg,
is a rosary, lilac in color.
O I could wring her—

In a sense,
Mother is a lover
of incense and usefulness,
Eastern European among other things.
Thick with the accent,
her friend is in her seventies: peacock feathers, green hat,
lots of rouge, and a Masters in Library Science.
They are coming over to see what is wrong with me.

Alison Kolodinsky

march

> *... a border region.*
> —Webster's dictionary

You said you were ready
for letting go when death
squirmed above his bed

like a cottonmouth
breaking the mirrored skin
of the river. But

how could you predict
that only seconds
after he'd been gone

the air lock of his room would
collapse, that your lungs
would spill a vulgar sound

and by taking the next
inevitable breath, you'd know
what it was to be let go.

In Carroll County, New Hampshire

for Laura

Unable to find ourselves
on a brand new accordion map of New Hampshire
we decide to stop
at a crossroad to walk through a graveyard
and patronize ancestors.

Evergreens tower around us
on three sides as we wander
in and out the rows of tombstones
rows like pews with a grassy aisle
long overgrown, down the center.

Crickets are tuning up
anxious to begin on this windless summer
evening. We bat mosquitoes, bees,
and kneel by the oldest
headstone so far. Slowly, I decipher:

> *SACRED*
> *To the memory of the*
>
> **HON. JOHN M. PAGE**
> *born at Deerfield, N.H. Feb.16.1778.*
> *and died May 15.1826. of a*
> *malignant fever which proved*
> *fatal to 5 children & himself in*
> *the short span of 8 weeks.*

Five small markers pull our faces
to the left, like magnets. We whisper
each child's name in disbelief
then retreat, each to herself.
I count again, to be sure,

calculate their little ages to
figure out the order in which the fever
took them. On the other side
buried beside her husband, is Dolly
who lived without them for forty more years.

I stand in the aisle and watch
her watching each procession—neighbors
shouldering her coffins, nearly
one a week. I imagine I'm Dolly
left behind to endure.

I see her turn away
as I turn away, and wonder
Can you hear me, Widow Page?
Tell me how, for the rest of her nights,
does a woman bed down with that faceless visitor?

Absence

Before your adoption, you and I lived
apart like stones
in the same dry riverbed, waiting
for someone to throw us together.

Now they say *absence seizures*—
some visible, some not—can steal you
when they want.
                  I follow you
everywhere, secretly
timing your daydreams, your speech,
the void between breaths as you fall
to sleep. At your age

I camped at Cove Palisades
a few treacherous miles from the gorge
of the Crooked River. One night
all the men formed a human
chain to look for a little boy
who'd wandered off in search of
the perfect marshmallow stick.

My mother zipped up the walls of the sky-
colored tent around us. At dusk,
with flashlights on, we played Old Maid
while the boy's mother
screamed his name, climbing the ridge on
all fours.

This is how it will be then,
until enough medicine
quenches your restless brain—if I
gesture and your eyes don't
track me, if my words escape
in the air between us,

I will wait like the mother of that child
whose name I've never been able
to recall.
        He was found
days later, alert, beside the river
at the base of Rocking Chair,
the highest cliff in that canyon
long since flooded
and dammed.

Inventing the Wind

for Rick

I open the windows wide to catch this spring
night as shadows press, darkening the silver
mustache of sedge that skims the Tomoka River
where baldcypresses wade in. I invent something

light to finger the balcony wind chimes,
to tease the spider webs linking the hammock,
something sudden—a wildcat
wind to ease the swamp, to stoke the fireflies

patrolling our maze of magnolia and oak,
just a breeze to lull the bullfrogs' *jug-o-rum,
jug-o-rum,* something long to quiet the hum
of the ceiling fan, something cool as a calypso.

I trace your lips with my finger, light as a veil,
while you dream, embracing the sheet, the sail.

Peter Schmitt

Glance

It happens hundreds of times each year
in the South, those nights before or after
the hottest of the summer. Someone
will be walking in the direction of home
after closing down a bar,
his body heat lifting
like his troubles
so completely and momentarily
from the insurge of alcohol,
that the warmth of the smooth paved road
stretching before him
will reach out like a familiar bed
or lover and take him in its arms
to sleep. She might have been
just accepting that invitation,
there in the middle of the street,
where the trees arched
and formed a tunnel. In the brief
cone of my headlights she was holding
to the ribbon of yellow paint, and in the flash
of our eyes meeting she seemed not frozen
like an animal, but lost, looking
for something. In a second's swerve
I was past her, yet managed to fix her
once in the mirror, till the road curved
and she vanished. And in no version
of her life will I ever come that close—
at best once backward glance, then gone.

A Day at the Beach

If he had been paying more attention
to whatever my mother was saying
from under her hat beneath the umbrella,

or watching more closely over my brother,
off playing somewhere with his shovel and pail,
or me, idly tracing my name in the sand,

if he hadn't had that faraway look,
gazing out to where the freighters crawled along
the horizon—so that when he suddenly

pushed up and off, sand in his wake, visor
taking wing behind him, you could believe,
as he churned toward the glassy water,

that it had just come to him to chuck it all,
this whole idea of family, and make
for those southbound freighters and the islands—

then he might never have seen the arm heaved up,
the lifeguards running just as my father
was lifting the old man out of the surf

and bearing him ashore, the blue receding
from his cramped limbs. And as a crowd closed around
the gasping figure struggling to his knees,

my father turned back to us—sheepishly,
almost, back to the endless vigilance
of husband and of father, which was all

he had ever asked for in the first place.

Under Desks

Was it 1966? —a bell would ring,
and we dropped to our knees, meshing fingers

above our heads in mixed-up prayer. Papers
would still be sliding down the sloping desktops,

gouged with names, curses, and pierced hearts, and a book
might slip off suddenly, and thud to the floor.

In our peripheral vision we could see
other shoesoles, elbows, and coming down

the aisle Mrs. Rayfield's pumps (why wasn't she
under her desk too?) —then a second bell rang,

and bumping our heads on the metal belly
bulging like an airplane's, we came back up,

to a world and lives we could not practice for,
where just hours later, beneath those same desks,

we might be passing notes (an intricate
network of spies already), *Who loved Whom*,

our missives betraying, evidently,
no sense of pending mortality, unless

it fueled their urgency. So much of what
we've managed to forget first came to us

above a schoolroom desk, so much of what
we've never quite learned happened lower down,

at knee-level, it was under desks we first
received our most dangerous assignments.

Homecoming

It sounds so much like joy,
the boisterous honking of the geese returning,
coming back to the lake.

It always catches us unprepared,
at our desk or in the garden,
like uninvited, but always welcome guests.

Moving to the window, or turning
to wipe a brow, we watch their long-held
chevron or arrowhead descend,

to take a triumphant lap around
the lake. The water will be stretched
like foil, the sun glinting gold into the trees.

We know this feeling ourselves,
arriving home after a long vacation,
and pushing the horn to nothing

but an empty house. So we pause
from our afternoon tasks and watch
this renewal of old intimacies,

the geese testing the water,
the dock, the small pebbly shore.
By the time we are standing

on the little beach, the honking
all around us now, we hope that,
in some way, they are glad to see us too.

But it doesn't matter. More
and more of them are sliding
out of the sky, coming back,

and all making noise, so that the joy
we feel is in ourselves—
standing by a lake in very late summer,

as another season
rounds the sun
perfectly on schedule.

Tin Ear

We stood at attention as she moved
with a kind of Groucho shuffle
down our line, her trained music
teacher's ear passing by
our ten- and eleven-year-old mouths
open to some song now forgotten.
And as she held her momentary
pause in front of me, I peered
from the corner of my eye
to hers, and knew the truth
I had suspected.
In the following days,
as certain of our peers
disappeared at appointed hours
for the Chorus, something in me
was already closing shop.
Indeed, to this day
I still clam up
for the National Anthem
in crowded stadiums, draw
disapproving alumni stares
as I smile the length of school songs,
and even hum and clap
through *Happy Birthday*, creating
a diversion—all lest I send
the collective pitch
careening headlong into dissonance.
It's only in the choice acoustics
of shower and sealed car
that I can finally give voice
to that heart deep within me
that is pure, tonally perfect, music.
But when the water stops running
and the radio's off, I can remember
that day in class,

when I knew for the first time
that mine would be a world of words
without melody, where *refrain*
means *do not join*,
where I'm ready to sing
in a key no one has ever heard.

Susan Mitchell

From the Journals of the Frog Prince

In March I dreamed of mud
sheets of mud over the ballroom chairs and table
rainbow slicks of mud under the throne.
In April I saw mud of clouds and mud of sun.
Now in May I find excuses to linger in the kitchen
for wafts of silt and ale
cinnamon and riverbottom
tender scallion and sour underlog.

At night I cannot sleep.
I am listening for the dribble of mud
climbing the stairs to our bedroom
as if a child in a wet bathing suit ran
up and down them in the dark.

Last night I said: Face it you're bored!
How many times can you live over with the same excitement
that moment when the princess leans
into the well her face a petal
falling to the surface of the water
as you rise like a bubble to her lips
the golden ball bursting from your mouth?
To test myself I said
remember how she hurled you against the wall
your body cracking open
skin shriveling to the bone
your small green heart splitting like a pod
and her face imprinted with every moment
of your transformation?

I no longer tremble.

Night after night I lie beside her.
"Why is your forehead so cool and damp?" she asks.
Her breasts are soft and dry as flour.
The hand that brushes my head is feverish.
At her touch I long for wet leaves
the slap of water against rocks.

"What are you thinking of?" she asks.
How can I tell her
I am thinking of the green skin
shoved like wet pants behind the Directoire desk?
Or tell her I am mortgaged to the hilt
of my sword, to the leek green tip of my soul?
Someday I will drag her by her hair
to the river—and what? Drown her?
Show her the green flame of my self rising at her feet?
But there's no more violence in her
than in a fence or a gate.

"What are you thinking of?" she whispers.
I am staring into the garden.
I am watching the moon
wind its trail of golden slime around the oak,
over the stone basin of the fountain.
How can I tell her
I am thinking that transformations are not forever?

Havana Birth

Off Havana, the ocean is green this morning
of my birth. The conchers clean their knives on leather
straps and watch the sky while three couples
who have been dancing on the deck of a ship
in the harbor, the old harbor of the fifties, kiss
each other's cheeks and call it a night.

On a green sofa five dresses wait
to be fitted. The seamstress kneeling at Mother's feet
has no idea I am about to be born. Mother
pats her stomach which is flat
as the lace mats on the dressmaker's table. She thinks
I'm playing in my room. But as usual, she's wrong.

I'm about to be born in a park in Havana. Oh,
this is important, everything in the dressmaker's house
is furred like a cat. And Havana leans right up
against the windows. In the park, the air
is chocolate, the sweet breath of a man
smoking an expensive cigar. The grass

is drinkable, dazzling, white. In a moment
I'll get up from a bench, lured
by a flock of pigeons, lazily sipping
the same syrupy music through a straw.
Mother is so ignorant, she thinks
I'm rolled like a ball of yarn under the bed. What

does she know of how I got trapped in my life?
She thinks it's all behind her, the bloody
sheets, the mirror in the ceiling
where I opened such a sudden furious blue, her eyes
bruised shut like mine. The pigeon's eyes
are orange, unblinking, a doll's. Mother always said

I wanted to touch everything because

I was a child. But I was younger than that.
I was so young I thought whatever I
wanted, the world wanted too. Workers
in the fields wanted the glint of sun on their machetes.
Sugarcane came naturally sweet, you

had only to lick the earth where it grew.
The music I heard each night outside
my window lived in the mouth of a bird. I was so young
I thought it was easy as walking
into the ocean which always had room
for my body. So when I held out my hands

I expected the pigeon to float between them
like a blossom, dusting my fingers with the manna
of its wings. But the world is wily, and doesn't want
to be held for long, which is why
as my hands reached out, workers lay down
their machetes and left the fields, which is why

a prostitute in a little *calle* of Havana dreamed
the world was a peach and flicked
open a knife. And Mother, startled, shook
out a dress with big peonies splashed like dirt
across the front, as if she had fallen
chasing after me in the rain. But what could I do?

I was about to be born, I was about to have
my hair combed into the new music
everyone was singing. The dressmaker sang it, her mouth
filled with pins. The butcher sang it and wiped
blood on his apron. Mother sang it and thought her body
was leaving her body. And when I tried

I was so young the music beat right
through me, which is how the pigeon got away.
The song the world sings day after day
isn't made of feathers, and the song a bird pours
itself into is tough as a branch
growing with the singer and the singer's delight.

The Kiss

He said I want to kiss you in a way
no one has ever kissed you before, a kiss
so special you will never forget and no one will ever

we had moved into a room away
from the others where coats were piled
on a bed, and in the almost dark the kiss began
to assume baroque proportions, expanding
and contracting like a headache   pushing winglike

from my feet. In adolescent fantasies I used to
think of myself in the third
person so that when I kissed for the first
time in a film of my own making a voice
kept saying Now he is kissing her, now she is
unbuttoning her blouse, now his hand

the voice just ahead of the picture or the sex
lagging always behind as in a badly
dubbed film   the voice

trying clumsily to undress them, hiding
behind a screen or hovering above the bed dovelike
a Holy Spirit of invention presiding over each
nipple, enticing erect the body's
erectile tissue, inflaming their eyes

to see in the dark hiddenness
of wordless doing, to watch, to keep watching
to the edge of, the verging precipice beyond which
language, thought's emissary huffing
and puffing, or beyond which language's undercover
agent and spy, thought. Now thinking back to
that time, I am always just behind myself
like a shadow, I am muteness
about to blossom   into mystic vision   or with some word

stick a pin into, fasten like a butterfly
on black velvet, though it seems forever since I
kissed the back of my hand, pretending
my hand was my mouth, my mouth
the man's, in order to know what a kiss was, teeth
gently pulling at the skin on top
near the knuckles, the way a cat lifts
its kitten by the nape of the neck, dragging it
to a dark place under a house, or

licking the inside of my hand up the heart
line, down the life line   I don't

remember who left the room first, though
when someone told me he was
a famous director, I watched more intently
as he held out a canapé
to his wife.
                Sometimes in the years
that followed I thought of him, his ornate
description of the kiss, which with time became
more ornate, his tongue glossing

the whorls and bric-a-brac, the Adirondack
antlers on the grotesque banquettes, the kiss
coiling round itself like a snail

a small Gongoresque affair with all its
engines thrumming, that description the most
memorable thing about him whose face, if I ever
really looked at it, I have forgotten,
whose mouth, whose teeth, whose tongue
did not open anything in me
but directly

presented themselves as one takes a pear or apple
into one's hand and walks down the street
not thinking about the apple
or pear, but simply eating.

Hunt Hawkins

Skating

In the dank, gray cinder block roller-rink,
their chrysalis, the subteens swarm.
The "cute" boy, shirttails flying, speeds
through a chain of four girls, breaking
their grip, rough, producing loads of giggles,
the minds of all dark but knowing somehow
of the fantastic change about to come.
The rental skates are tough as army boots,
sweat-stained uppers, polyurethane wheels chipped
by generations probably going back to Plato.
Here and there a few adults skate,
mostly propping up smaller children
as mares nuzzle their foals to stand, but
I notice one gray-haired man with a woman,
his daughter, fighting. Is she deaf? Retarded?
She can't speak. He has the exasperated
look of a man life has called to be a saint
when he didn't really feel like it.
He should be thinking retirement, trips
to Hawaii, but instead has to worry how
this daughter will survive when he ceases to be.
She is pale, unnaturally. Skinny. She waves
freckled stick arms in his face, demanding
God knows what, until he sits on a bench,
crosses his legs, his mind rolling over
some hard floor of knowledge.
Finally she gives up, moves into the
careening crowd—but she is brilliant,
cruising smoothly among the subteenagers,
on the turns laying one foot over the other
like jumping checkers, sure, relaxed

from a lifetime of weekly outings. When
she passes his sullen bench, she waves
to her dad, but as she circles, her hands
linger strangely by her face, a palm
by each cheek, fluttering spasmodically
like a butterfly trying to be born.

Honeymoon

When we pick up our marriage license,
the Commonwealth of Pennsylvania, full of wisdom,
gives us a plastic bag of promotional gifts
deemed useful to wedded life:
a roll of Tums, a bottle of Windex, two dozen aspirin.
As we drive to the Delaware coast,
my wife finds the true treasure
nestled at the bottom of the bag,
a paperback picturing a dark-haired girl on a cliff,
her white dress blowing in the wind, *The Zephyrs of Love*.
For the next two days we hardly leave the room.
We don't even bother to dress.
Instead we take turns reading the book aloud.
It seems the poor English girl, Dominique,
was forced to marry a Greek shipping tycoon
with a scar across his face
because her father owed him lots of money.
She hated Petros with his arrogant ways
and ugly disfiguration
until one night he slipped into her room.
Slowly he ran his swarthy hand
under Dominique's satin nightgown.
When she woke to protest,
he shouted, "But you're my wife!"
As Dominique struggled futilely,
an animal passion seized her soul.
My wife and I stare at each other,
then at my scars:
the knee with the cartilage operation
and the finger I cut on a beer can.
We've taken years to decide to marry,
and we're still not completely sure.
How do Dominique and Petros do it?
They quickly resolve all their differences
as Petros forgives her father's debt
and reveals he received his scar

fighting the Nazis in the Resistance.
Our honeymoon is over.
I think my wife and I are ready
for the Windex, Tums, and aspirin,
knowing our lives will never shine
with the wonderful light of inevitability.
That's all right.
As we take a last walk down the beach,
I practice shouting, "But you're my wife!"

The Prejohn

Last night at the movie theater,
going to relieve myself,
I kept thinking what a hard day
Adam must have had
when he was obliged to name all those animals:
kangaroo, porcupine, protozoa, drosophila, and on and on.
That must be why so many things
remain unnamed;
for example, the little room you enter
before you get to the bathroom.
I paused there, puzzled, pondering—
and hoping no one would come in and get the wrong impression.
What's the purpose of this room? You say
it's so outsiders of the different gender
don't catch any untoward sights,
but clearly we don't need a whole room for that—
just a crook or partition.
Why have prejohns
when we don't have precars or prekitchens?
I examined the room carefully.
It had bright lights, flowered wallpaper, white moldings.
I've had friends who lived in worse places than this!
And think of the thousands of prejohns across the country,
empty, going to waste.
We should at least put in shelves
and use them to store jams and jellies.
Or they could house refugees
from countries less fortunate and democratic than our own.
Or we could chain a prisoner in each one.
That way, not only would we relieve prison overcrowding,
but we'd provide a warning against crime
to every citizen going to take a whiz.
But something's wrong here.
It's the room itself we should get rid of.
We've all become Greta Garbos
in our quest for privacy.

We've become islands, not part of the main.
Why do we even need a bathroom
to go to the bathroom?
Shouldn't we be more like Adam's animals,
innocent and free, urinating in the wind,
defecating in the fields,
returning what we don't need
to great Nature from which it came?
O, yes, yes, shouldn't we be more like the French?

Apnea

My infant son, Samuel, sleeps in his crib,
hunched forward like a small Mohammedan,
while I watch in the dark room,
unable to sleep, listening to his breathing.
The doctors say we all stop many times
each night, but decide to start again.
Two miles away the trucks on the interstate
sizzle. I realize how hard it is
not to think of myself as watched,
if only by some small man inside my head
who keeps everything going. Does he have
a little cot in there, does he ever sleep?
Outside a confused mockingbird starts to sing
long before dawn. The furnace goes on and off,
keeping the house warm. A bit later
the refrigerator does the same, a countermove.
Samuel's chest keeps heaving. Maybe
the world just happens, but sometimes it doesn't.
I can see I will spend the rest of my life
hoping my son will want to breathe.

Pennies

In the 7-11 I buy milk,
get three cents back and wonder:
what can I make of my change,
the three dark spots in my palm.
Once these well-muscled citizens
did the nation's work: they were sunburnt
Scotch-Irish plowing Nebraska, sooty Welshmen
descending the coalmines of Pennsylvania,
African ex-slaves picking Alabama's cotton.
They were round and carried on their backs
the bearded, warty face of a President
who believed in government of, by, and for
the people. Now they are nothing,
the empty hoof-marks of an economy
which has galloped away.
What happened to sweated labor?
Doesn't anyone make anything any more?
Our thoroughbred corporations just
throw them aside. They fill jars
on bedroom bureaus, piled roughly
in miserable ghettoes.
They sit idly in cups next to
cash-registers with signs saying:
"Got one, leave one; need one, take one."
They have been replaced by silver-colored money:
aristocratic Kennedy half-dollars,
fat bourgeois quarters, little Yuppie dimes,
ever anxious lower-middle class nickles.
O poor pennies! Displaced workers! Despised citizens!
All you are good for now is
to litter the bottoms of wishing wells
and to cover the eyes of the dead.

Stephen Gibson

American Primitive

The lion does not rule the lamb in Hicks'
Peaceable Kingdom, but looks out with eyes
serene with wonder from the plane of the painting.
When the rapture comes, the lion is saying,
it will look like this—like the painting hung
in the Everson Museum, one version of the hundred
Hicks painted. Like *idiot savants*,
who calculate the roots of enormous numbers
or who can play a Bach requiem as soon
as they hear it, the painting has all of the power
of the very simple. But encoded in those songs
Hicks' birds send out, from leafy tree-top
to wheat-colored meadow, are messages
only the romantic or religious—armed
with their fanatical evasions and denials—
refuse to acknowledge: last week
a horse kicked my neighbor's boy in the stomach,
perforated his liver and collapsed a lung.
Now, after his third operation, his mother
speaks to his unconscious, hoping she soothes him.
Last night, my friend called to tell me
his wife had left him, that he felt dead
inside, but now he had to think of his daughter.
Hicks, those birds never have known a worm
called conscience; and as for values,
their songs are posted warnings to others,
"Trespassers, Keep Out." And those pretty Indians
you've drawn, about to conclude a treaty
with Penn in the background—in this world
they won't be giving up what they can still hang onto.

The Bacchae: The Deaths of Benito Mussolini and Claretta Petacci, Milan, April 29, 1945

A last night together, then execution in Dongo
(ever the showman, Mussolini bared his chest
to the bullets, which struck, instead, his mistress
Claretta Petacci); then the drive to Piazzale Loreto
where the bodies were dumped. He who had compelled
a nation to imitate the Bersaglieri trot
of army maneuvers, did not see converging on the spot,
first the curious, then, the enraged. The crowd swelled.

Led by a few faint hearts, the dead were taunted:
weak stuff—smacks, punches, a kick to the head.
It was not enough. Women who had once kissed
his portrait now squatted over him and pissed—
that was better. The corpses were strung up. (Someone
noticed that Claretta's stockings hadn't even a run.)

The Bra

As my wife buys our daughter her first bra
I wait beside the escalator
with our packages from Sears and J.C. Penney's,
and think of what Balthus meant
when he denied the erotic in his paintings—
who saw only the pubescent form
in its undevelopment, whether nude before a mirror
or clothed, reading, one leg over an armchair;
to which one critic argues
Balthus invites the reader to complete such content,
the dreaminess of adolescence
whose adventures are in daydreaming, in reading books
or in listening to the radio
while waiting for the real adventures to begin
(hopeful, and therefore innocent—
which Balthus thought his content—
because they do not yet know what it is that *we* know).
No, there is nothing of the erotic
in the awkward adolescent leaning forward on her elbow,
in her skirt, reading the newspaper on the floor,
or in the girl, asleep, spread-eagled on a chaise
and her cat lapping from a bowl of milk.

The Answer

That tapestries with unicorns and young girls petting them
are medieval fact, or that revolutionaries
warmed potatoes in them (also fact) during the Terror,
are details that mean nothing and are unknown to my daughter,
who's taken me to Ringling's version of this sexual lore—
father and daughter to meet a goat in make-up.
That it's smart business is proved at the ticket counter.
But it so happens, on the auditorium door
is the photo of a girl abducted last year,
taken by a blue van, who hasn't been found.
Like the hundreds whose faces appear on milk cartons.
Like the hundreds more waiting in turn.
And I'm in no mood as the house lights darken;
my thoughts are elsewhere, with a blue van.
I don't tell her that they cut its horns,
then grafted one that rooted in its forehead.
I don't tell her Ringling is a fraud,
any more than that virgins can take a beast to bed
and not bleed a little. But the world's no riddle
though we'd like to think so. So in the middle
of the one question from the only daughter
I will ever have, I tell her it's not water
or fairy powder that's sprinkled on its coat.
It's chopped aluminum. And I tell her it's a goat.

Sharon Weightman

My Children Know Reggae

My children know reggae.
My son sings *buffalo soldier*.
My daughter sings *no woman no cry*.
Together they sing about red, red wine.

My son, who is nine,
has climbed a tree in the mountains of Jamaica
to bring down a shirtful of alligator pears.
My daughter, who is fourteen,
was kissed for the very first time
on a porch in Mandeville.
It was sunset, she says,
the sky was red as blood,
and Auntie Janice was watching through the window
with a funny smile.

My children know reggae.
Their cousins taught them to dance in Coconut Grove
with the pelvic rock that affirms
this world's center of gravity.
They listen to handed-down tapes
and scratched LP's in white paper sleeves,
long separated from the album covers
of black, yellow, green and red,
so that the only images they have
are the ones the music makes in their minds.

My friend Alice has sent me
an invitation to a dance.
She and her family are celebrating
Bob Marley's birthday. The card mentions

that he died at thirty-three.
In his honor, hundreds of people
will dance and drink wine.

My children know reggae
but they don't know history.
My daughter asks me
what Bob Marley died from.
I don't know the answer,
but I want to say heartbreak.
Instead, I tell her I'll ask Auntie Janice,
I'm sure she'll know.
My son asks me if he was a black man.
Of course, I say, surprised at the question.
I thought so, he says slowly.
Black men die young, don't they?
It seems like black men die young.

I know the answer to this one,
but I don't want to give it.
I want to reassure him
every little thing's gonna be all right.
In the silence that follows,
he asks another question:
Why were they called the Wailers anyway?

A Prayer for My Quadroon Daughter

a response to Yeats

I won't wish back your beauty, though strangers are
Distraught by it. In stores they stop to stare
At you; they buy you gum, a candy bar;
They cannot keep their hands from your black hair.
I wish that it were easier to trust them.
At three it's easy to delight the world.
But give your heart with caution, caution. Custom
Has an easy answer for high yellow girls.
I cannot even wish you innocence.
Why would I lead the rabbit to the snare?
Be devious, street-wise, wary, obstinate:
Dark things are peddled on the thoroughfare.
There is no hill, no tower that can hide you.
Root yourself deep. Every wind will find you.

Sharon Weightman

On Monroe Street

                              here
where a man pisses in the phone booth
in front of the Temple of Holy Fire   here
where kids nod in the alley
between Fat Daddy's Car Cleaners
and the Day and Nite Cafe   here
where I would lie   steal   whore
to get my children out of here
where so many women
do it and do it
and are still here
where a woman has painted
the front of this tall house
bottom-of-the-swimming-pool blue
the sides still splintering
gray as cinderblock   here
where things learn to grow in the shade
a woman has lined her porch
with spiky green shoots in rusty cans   here
where sweet potato vines in plastic hanging baskets
are climbing out of the tired dirt
snaking their way to sun   here
where a woman has clothes-pinned
white uniforms to a rigged-up line   here
where the dirt is a hundred years old
a woman is sweeping the second story porch   here
where it is no use as far as I can see
a woman is sweeping
where a broom will reach

Night Song

Nothing about you is easy.
The years turn around
without your help.
Women put their dreams to bed.
When two lie down
to sleep, you are not there.
It doesn't matter where
you were once. Bone
crushes to powder in your hand.
You won't give the dark
what it wants.
Sometimes you wonder what
will compass you. You're tired
of your own passions.
Why doesn't your blood break
out from under your fingernails?
Your tongue tastes only
salt, skin. You pretend
you want to continue
in the middle of things.
Something propels you
through the night. You sleep
too late to write aubades.
You want to begin. You want to end.

In Time

the truth isn't worth telling
we say that
       in time
acts burn down
to the bone of good intention
we can't quite remember
when we forgot discretion

we say that
time makes us innocent
       in time
we even say it with conviction
thinking of the jury
over and over
composing our plea

Biographical Notes

Judith Berke's first book, *White Morning*, was published by Wesleyan University Press in 1989. A chapbook, *Acting Problems*, came out from Silverfish Review Press in 1993. She is currently completing two manuscripts: one titled *Against Gravity* and the other, on the paintings of Van Gogh, as yet untitled. She received a Florida Individual Artist Fellowship in 1989.

Van K. Brock's poems have appeared in such journals as *Iowa Review*, *The New Yorker*, and *The Southern Review*, and in such anthologies as *The New Yorker Book of Poems*; *Strong Measures* (Phil Dacey and David Allen Evans, eds.: Harper & Row); *The Made Thing* (Leon Stokesbury, ed.: Arkansas); *Blood to Remember: American Poets on the Holocaust* (Charles Fishman, ed.: Texas Tech); and *Sweet Nothings: The Poetry of Rock'n'Roll* (Elledge, Indiana). His collections include *The Hard Essential Landscape* (Contemporary Poetry Series, University Presses of Florida). His essay, "Images of Elvis, the South, and America," is in *Elvis: Images and Fancies* (University Press of Mississippi and W.H. Allen, Ltd., London). As editor of *International Quarterly*, his editorial essays have ranged from his experiences in Eastern Europe, African drama as witness, the aftermath of colonialism in Asia, and the diversity of the Americas. He is founder and President of Anhinga Press, Inc., and teaches poetry writing and literature at Florida State University. He received Florida Individual Artist Fellowships in 1977 and in 1982.

Rick Campbell lives in Gadsden County, Florida, with his wife Marcia and their new baby, Della Rose. He teaches English at Florida A&M University. In 1994 he received an NEA Fellowship in poetry and he has received two Florida Individual Artist Fellowships (1986 and 1993). His work has appeared in many journals such as *The Georgia Review*, *The Missouri Review*, and *The Ohio Review*. His poems will soon appear in *Southern Poetry Review* and *Prairie Schooner*. He has published two hard-to-find chapbooks, *Driving to Wyoming* (1981) and *The Breathers at St. Marks* (1994).

G.S. Sharat Chandra is an internationally-known fiction writer and poet. Some of his stories and poems have appeared in *The Paris Review*, *The Partisan Review*, *Short Story International*, *Poetry*, and *The London Magazine*. A former senior Fulbright in Creative Writing and winner of an NEA Fellowship in Creative Writing, Chandra has given readings at the Library of Congress, Oxford, and McDaid's Pub in Dublin. He received a Florida Individual Artist Fellowship in 1980. He is the author of eight books, including translations from the Sanskrit and from English into the Indian language Kannada. His latest books are *Family of Mirrors* (BkMk Press, Missouri, 1993) and *Immigrants of Loss* (Hippopotamus Press, U.K., 1993-94).

Biographical Notes

Joanne Childers was born in Cincinnati, Ohio, and has lived in Gainesville, Florida, since receiving her M.A. in Modern European History from the University of Florida. Her poems have appeared in *The Georgia Review, The Florida Review, Massachusetts Review, Sewanee Review*, and many other journals, as well as textbooks published by Harcourt-Brace and Simon and Schuster. She received a Florida Individual Artist Fellowship in 1980. She has published two books: *The Long Distance* and *Moving Mother Out*.

Stephen Corey is the author of six volumes of poetry including *All These Lands You Call One Country* (University of Missouri Press, 1992) and *Synchronized Swimming* (Swallow's Tales Press, 1985). He is currently the Associate Editor of *The Georgia Review*. His poems, essays, and reviews have appeared in *The American Poetry Review, Poetry, The Kenyon Review, Ploughshares, The North American Review*, and *The Ohio Review*. His work has been published in a number of anthologies, including *The Pushcart Prize IX* (1984). In 1992 and 1993 he was selected as the Georgia Author of the Year in Poetry by the Georgia Council of Writers and Journalists. He received a Florida Individual Artist Fellowship in 1979.

Silvia Curbelo was born in Matanzas, Cuba, in 1955 and emigrated to the U.S. in 1967. She has received a Florida Individual Artist Fellowship (1989), poetry fellowships from the NEA and the Cintas Foundation, and an Atlantic Center for the Arts Cultural Exchange Fellowship to La Napoule Arts Foundation in France. She was co-winner of the 1992 James Wright Poetry Prize from *Mid-American Review*, and was recently awarded an "Escape to Create" fellowship from the Seaside Institute. A collection of poems, *The Geography of Leaving*, was published by Silverfish Review Press in 1991. Her work has appeared in *Kenyon Review, Yellow Silk, Prairie Schooner, Indiana Review, Bloomsbury Review* and many other publications.

Laurence Donovan, poet and graphic artist, is a retired professor of English at the University of Miami, Coral Gables, Florida, where he taught courses in contemporary literature and creative writing. He has published poems and drawings in many of the better literary magazines and has illustrated numerous small press chapbooks by such writers as Donald Justice, Tram Combs and Ronald Perry. He received a Florida Individual Artist Fellowship in 1983. His poems have twice been included in the *Borestone Mountain Best Poems* anthologies, and a chapbook by Laurence Lieberman, *The Monkeys of St. Kitts*, including two of his illustrations, is forthcoming from Cummington Press.

Stephen Gibson's poems and short fiction have appeared in *Poetry, Western Humanities Review, New England Review, Mississippi Review, Ironwood, The Southern Review, Quarterly West, New Orleans Review, Fiction,* and several other journals. He teaches at Palm Beach Community College and lives in Royal Palm Beach with his wife, Clorinda, and their two children, Kyla and Joseph. He received a Florida Individual Artist Fellowship in 1994.

Dean Gioia feels that his greatest accomplishment as an artist may be that he has lived exclusively from the sale of his work for more than 20 years. Gioia received a Florida Individual Artist Fellowship for Visual Arts/Painting in 1989; he has exhibited widely in the Southeast, and his work is held in more than 300 public, corporate, and private collections throughout the United States. His primary focus as a painter is the use of light and atmosphere to explore the ethereal nature of the Florida landscape.

Barbara Hamby is a poet, fiction writer, and editor. Her collection of poetry, *Delirium*, won the 1994 Vassar Miller Prize and will be published by the University of North Texas Press in 1995. Her poems have appeared in *The Iowa Review*, *The Paris Review*, *Western Humanities Review*, *Negative Capability*, and other magazines. She received a Florida Individual Artist Fellowship in 1988.

Peter Hargitai is winner of the American Academy of Poets Translation Award, the Milan Füst Prize from the Hungarian Academy of Arts and Sciences, a Fulbright, and a Florida Individual Artist Fellowship (1990). He publishes poetry and fiction in both English and Hungarian.

Sam Harrison has been writing and publishing poems and short fiction for a quarter-century. He has written two novels, *Walls of Blue Coquina* and *Birdsong Ascending*, both published by Harcourt Brace Jovanovich. He lives at the beach, somewhere between Ormond and Flagler. He received a Florida Individual Artist Fellowship in 1982.

Lola Haskins has published five books of poetry: *Planting the Children* (University Press of Florida 1983), *Castings* (Countryman Press 1984, Betony Press, 1992), *Across Her Broad Lap Something Wonderful* (State Street Press 1989), *Forty-Four Ambitions for the Piano* (University Press of Florida 1990, Betony Press 1994), and *Hunger* (University of Iowa Press 1993). Haskins has won a number of prizes for her work, including the Emily Dickinson Prize, the Madeline Sadin Award, and narrative poetry prizes from *New England Review/Breadloaf Quarterly* and *Southern Poetry Review*. *Hunger* was the 1992 winner of the Edwin Ford Piper Award from Iowa. She has held two Florida Individual Artist Fellowships (1979 and 1990) and has been an NEA Fellow. Since 1978 she has taught Computer Science at the University of Florida. She lives with her husband Gerald in an owner-built house on a farm outside Gainesville.

Biographical Notes

Hunt Hawkins's book of poetry, *The Domestic Life*, won the 1992 Agnes Lynch Starrett Prize and was published by the University of Pittsburgh Press in 1994. His poems have appeared in *The Georgia Review, The Southern Review, Poetry, the minnesota review,* and many other journals. He received a Florida Individual Artist Fellowship in 1993. He is Professor of English at Florida State University.

Donald Justice was born in Miami, Florida, in 1925. He is the author of more than seven books including *The Summer Anniversaries* (1959), *Night Light* (1967), *Departures* (1973), *Selected Poems* (1979, awarded the Pulitzer Prize in 1980), *The Sunset Maker* (1987), and *A Donald Justice Reader* (1992). His *New and Selected Poems* will be published in the fall of 1995. He is a four-time NEA Fellow and has received fellowships from the Rockefeller Foundation and the Guggenheim Foundation. In 1983 he received a Florida Individual Artist Fellowship. He was the co-winner of the Bollingen Prize in 1991. He has taught at a number of unversities, including Syracuse, Iowa, and the University of Florida. He currently lives in Iowa.

Brandon Kershner teaches creative writing and Modern British literature at the University of Florida. He has published books on Dylan Thomas and James Joyce, and edited several more on Joyce. His poetry has appeared in *The Georgia Review, Tampa Review, Poetry,* and other journals, and he published a chapbook, *Several Dialogues*, in collaboration with the photographer Todd Walker. He has also translated the Dutch poet Elly de Waard and collaborated on the first translations of Dylan Thomas into Roumanian. He received a Florida Individual Artist Fellowship in 1980.

David Kirby is W. Guy McKenzie Professor of English at Florida State University, where he has won three awards for teaching. A recipient of two Florida Individual Artist Fellowships (1983 and 1989) and a fellowship from the NEA, he is the author or editor of sixteen books, including *Saving the Young Men of Vienna*, which won the University of Wisconsin's Brittingham Prize in Poetry, and the forthcoming *Big-Leg Music*. He has published poems, reviews, and essays in such journals as *The New York Times Book Review, The Times Literary Supplement, The Village Voice, The Quarterly, The Southern Review, Sewanee Review,* and *Kenyon Review*.

Judith Kitchen is a regular reviewer of poetry for *The Georgia Review*. Her book, *Only the Dance: Essays on Time and Memory*, was published by the University of South Carolina Press in 1994. She has received a Pushcart Prize, an NEA Fellowship, and an award from the New York State Foundation for the Arts.

Jeffrey Knapp teaches English at Florida International University. He pioneered the Poets-in-the-Schools Program in South Florida (1974-89). He is the author of a chapbook, *The Acupuncture of Heaven*, and his translations of Felix Morisseau-Leroy's Haitian-Creole poetry are collected in *Haitia and Other Oddities*. He received a Florida Individual Artist Fellowship in 1978.

Alison Kolodinsky's poems have appeared in *Poetry, Kansas Quarterly, Cream City Review, Sing Heavenly Muse, The Panhandler*, and other journals and in several anthologies. She was a fellow at the Atlantic Center for the Arts in 1984 and in 1989; she received a Florida Individual Artist Fellowship in 1991.

Steve Kronen's poems, essays, and reviews have appeared in *American Poetry Review, The Paris Review, Poetry, The Georgia Review, Kenyon Review* and many other journals. His book, *Empirical Evidence*, was published in 1992 by University of Georgia Press and was a Contemporary Poetry Series winner. He has been a fellow at Bread Loaf and received a Florida Individual Artist Fellowship in 1989. He and his wife, fiction writer Ivonne Lamazares, are expecting their first child, Sophie, in July, 1995.

P.V. LeForge was born in Detroit, but has spent most of his life in Florida. After a fairly typical middle-class upbringing, he attended college, sold tires, racked steel, jobbed records and tapes, edited educational materials, and played semipro baseball. His book of stories, *The Principle of Interchange*, was published in 1990, and his book of poems, *The Secret Life of Moles*, appeared two years later. He received a Florida Individual Artist Fellowship in 1980. He currently lives in Tallahassee where he owns a bookstore specializing in fine literature and plays league tennis at the 4.5 level. A novel and a second book of poems are in the works.

Peter Meinke is the recent winner of the Paumanok Poetry Award (1993). Meinke has published four chapbooks as well as four books in the Pitt Poetry series. He has received two NEA Fellowships and three prizes from the Poetry Society of America, including the 1992 Emily Dickinson Award. He received Florida Individual Artist Fellowships in 1978 and in 1985. Meinke's poetry has appeared in *The New Yorker, The Atlantic, The Georgia Review*, and dozens of other magazines, and his collection of stories, *The Piano Tuner*, won the 1986 Flannery O'Connor Award. He was for many years the Director of the Creative Writing Program at Eckerd College. His most recent book is *Liquid Paper: New & Selected Poems*.

A. McA. Miller has edited *New Collage Magazine*, a Sarasota-based triquarterly of poetry and graphics, for twenty-five years now. He helped pioneer the "Voices and Visions" series in libraries statewide for the Florida Humanities Council. As Professor of Literature at New College of USF, he supplements his income by hosting Ruskin House Bed & Breakfast in Ruskin, Florida. He depletes his income by mail-outs of his work to magazines. He received a Florida Individual Artist Fellowship in 1983.

Susan Mitchell is a poet, editor, translator, essayist, and educator whose work has appeared in various journals and anthologies, including *American Poetry Review*, *The Atlantic*, *The New Yorker*, *Parnassus: Poetry in Review*, and *Best American Essays 1988*. Her translations of Dante appeared in *Versions of the Inferno*, edited by Daniel Halpern. She has published two books of poems, *Rapture* and *The Water Inside the Water*, with HarperCollins. She has received fellowships from the NEA, the Guggenheim Foundation, the Lannan Foundation. She received a Florida Individual Artist Fellowship in 1992. A finalist for the National Book Award, Mitchell has also received the Kingsley Tufts Award, two Pushcart Prizes, and the "Discovery"/*The Nation* award. Currently at work on a new volume of poems and a collection of essays, she teaches at Florida Atlantic University where she holds the Mary Blossom Lee endowed chair in Creative Writing.

W.C. Morton is from Winter Park, Florida. He received a Florida Individual Artist Fellowship in 1980.

Eugenie Nable lives and writes in Westchester County, New York. She received a Florida Individual Artist Fellowship in 1981.

Nancy Powell Rousseau has lived in Sitka, Alaska, for four years where she spends summers on a commercial salmon troller and winters wishing she were in Florida. Her poems have appeared in *Southern Poetry Review*, *Apalachee Quarterly*, *SunDog*, and other journals. She received a Florida Individual Artist Fellowship in 1981.

Christy Sheffield Sanford is a 1992 recipient of an NEA in literature (poetry). She has been awarded two Florida Individual Artist Fellowships, one for both Fiction and Poetry (1988) and one in the Interdisciplinary Category (1994). She is the author of five books: *Italian Smoking Piece* (Helicon Nine Editions, Kansas City, MO); *Bride Thrashing through History* (Bloody Twin Press, Stout, OH); *Only the Nude Can Redeem the Landscape* (Apalachee Press, Tallahassee, FL); *The Cowrie Shell Piece* (Flockophobic Press Ltd., New York, NY); and *The H's: The Spasms of a Requiem* (Bloody Twin Press, Stout, OH). She is currently a Visiting Writer at The University of Toledo.

Yvonne V. Sapia was born in New York City. Her family originally came from Puerto Rico. Sapia received a Bachelor of Arts from Florida Atlantic University, a Master of Arts from University of Florida, and a Doctor of Philosophy from Florida State University. She has been the recipient of an NEA Fellowship and two Florida Individual Artist Fellowships (1982 and 1987). Primarily a poet, her work has appeared in several anthologies and in numerous literary journals including *Carolina Quarterly*, *New Orleans Review*, *Partisan Review*, *Prairie Schooner*, and *The Southern Review*. Sapia has published two collections of poetry, *The Fertile Crescent* (Anhinga Press, 1983) and *Valentino's Hair* (Northeastern University Press, 1987), for which she received the Samuel French Morse Poetry Prize. In 1991 she received the Nilon Award for excellence in minority fiction, and her first novel, *Valentino's Hair*, was published by University of Colorado Press and Fiction Collective Two. She lives in rural North Florida.

Peter Schmitt's new book of poems, *Hazard Duty*, is forthcoming in Fall 1995 from Copper Beech Press, which brought out his first collection, *Country Airport*, in 1989. He is the recipient of a Florida Individual Artist Fellowship (1992), the Peter I.B. Lavan Younger Poets Award from the Academy of American Poets (selected by Richard Wilbur, 1991), the "Discovery"/*The Nation* Prize for Poetry (1988), and a supporting fellowship from the Ingram Merrill Foundation. His poems, reviews and essays have appeared in such publications as *The Georgia Review*, *The Miami Herald*, *The Nation*, *The Paris Review*, *Poetry*, *The Southern Review*, and a number of anthologies. Educated at Amherst College and the University of Iowa, he currently resides in his hometown of Miami, Florida.

Gail Shepherd is glad to be back in Florida: she thinks her great great granddaddy had the right idea when he moved here. Pittsburgh, San Francisco and London were too cold and rainy. She now edits and publishes *Red Herring*, a biweekly alternative arts rag in Palm Beach County. She is halfway through a novel, and her manuscript of poems, *First Questions*, is doing a tour of duty on the contest circuit. Shepherd received a Florida Individual Artist Fellowship in 1989.

Enid Shomer's stories and poems have appeared in *The New Yorker*, *The Atlantic*, *Poetry*, *Paris Review*, and other journals. Most recently, she is the author of *This Close to the Earth* (University of Arkansas Press, 1992), a collection of poems, and *Imaginary Men*, winner of the Iowa Short Fiction Award and the LSU/*Southern Review* Fiction Award given for the best first collection of short stories published by an American in 1993. Shomer was recently Writer-in-Residence at the Thurber House in Columbus, Ohio. Her new book of poems, *Black Drum*, is forthcoming. She received Florida Individual Artist Fellowships in 1985 and in 1991.

Edmund Skellings has been the Poet Laureate of the State of Florida since 1980. His books of poetry include, *Nearing the Millenium*, a trilogy from the University Presses of Florida. His publications include books, video poems, and multimedia works. In 1973 Skellings joined the faculty of Florida International University as the Director of the International

Biographical Notes

Institute for Creative Communication (IICC). His computer-assisted teaching programs, *Electric Poet* and *Comma Cat*, were re-published by IBM in 1985; *Scholastic Magazine* called *Comma Cat* "the best of the best." His most recent book, *Living Proof*, was published by the University Presses of Florida. In 1982 Skellings founded ARTNET, an arts and humanities microcomputer network. Articles on Skellings' inventions and innovations have appeared in *Time Life Books*, *PC Magazine*, and *Computer World*. He received a Florida Individual Artist Fellowship in 1980.

Hal Steven Shows is a poet and musician who lives in Tallahassee, Florida. A chapbook, *A Breath for Nothing*, was published by Anhinga Press in 1977. He received a Florida Individual Artist Fellowship in 1982. With the band "Persian Gulf" he produced three LPs and a solo effort, *Birthday Suit*, during the 1980s. His latest record, *Lifeboat*, was released in the spring of 1995.

Sharon Weightman, who received a Florida Individual Artist Fellowship in 1994, lives in Neptune Beach. She works as an arts reporter and columnist for the *Florida Times-Union*. Her poems have been published in *New York Quarterly*, *Plainswoman*, *Sojourner*, and other literary journals. She has received an Art Ventures Award for Poetry, was a playwrighting fellow at the Atlantic Center for the Arts, and was nominated for a Pushcart Prize by the *Beloit Poetry Journal*.

Acknowledgments

Berke: "The Strangler Fig" appeared in *New Letters*. "The Poem Beginning in the Bed of My Mother and Father" first appeared in *New Republic* and then in *White Morning* (Wesleyan University Press, 1989). "We Know Now" first appeared in *Partisan Review*. "Madrid Del Ovido" appeared in *Mangrove*. "Triple Toe Loop" appeared in *The Atlantic*. Reprinted by permission of the author.

Brock: "The Hindenberg" appeared in *New England Review*. "Epistle for the Cicadas" appeared in *Ploughshares*. "Sunday Morning with Prokofiev" first appeared in *The American Voice*. Reprinted by permission of the author.

Campbell: "Hanging Tobacco" was in *Cottonwood*. "Leaving Home, Pittsburgh, 1966" appeared in *Apalachee Quarterly*. "Ohio River Sunday" first appeared in *The Panhandler*. "The Geography of Desire" was published in *Tar River Poetry*. Reprinted by permission of the author.

Chandra: "Immigrants of Loss" is included in *Immigrants of Loss* (Hippopotamus Press, U.K., 1993-94). "Identities" first appeared in *Poet & Critic* and then, along with "Love Rites," in *Family of Mirrors* (BkMk Press, Missouri, 1993). "At the Burning-Ghats" appeared in *American Poetry Review*. Reprinted by permission of the author.

Childers: "Tracking Halley's Comet" appeared in *Kentucky Poetry Journal*. "Garden Touring with Aunt Mae" appeared in *Chattahoochee Review*. Reprinted by permission of the author.

Corey: "Belief" and "Deaf and Mute" were included in *Synchronized Swimming* (Swallow's Tale Press, 1985; reprinted by Livingston University Press, 1993). Copyright © 1985 by Stephen Corey. Reprinted by permission of the author.

Curbelo: "Bedtime Stories" and "The Lake has Swallowed the Whole Sky" appeared in *The Geography of Leaving* (Silverfish Review Press, 1991). "Last Call" appeared in *Tampa Review*. "Tonight I Can Almost Hear the Singing" appeared in *Kenyon Review*. "Drinking Song" and "Photograph of My Parents" appeared in *Prairie Schooner*. Reprinted by permission of the author.

Donovan: "Dog Island IX" appeared in *Spirit*. "The Traveler" appeared in *Cedarmere Review*. Reprinted by permission of the author.

Gibson: "American Primitive" and "The Answer" appeared in *Chelsea*. "The Bra" appeared in *The Paris Review*. "The Bacchae: The Deaths of Benito Mussolini and Claretta Petacci, Milan, April 29, 1945" appeared in

Acknowledgments

Apalachee Quarterly. Reprinted by permission of the author.

Hamby: "The Language of Bees" appeared in *Another Chicago Magazine*. "St. Anthony of the Floating Larynx" and "The Ovary Tattoo" appeared in *The Iowa Review*. Reprinted by permission of the author.

Hargitai: "The Art of Taxidermy" appeared in *Nimrod*. "Cats" appeared in *College English*. "Mother's Visit No. 29" appeared in *California Quarterly*. Reprinted by permission of the author.

Haskins: "The Prodigy" is included in *Forty-Four Ambitions for the Piano* (University Presses of Florida 1990; Betony Press 1994). "How I Learned" appeared in *The Southern Review*. "A Confluence" is included in *Hunger* (Iowa 1993). "Uchepas" appeared in *Ploughshares*. Reprinted by permission of the author.

Hawkins: "Honeymoon," "Apnea," "Pennies," "The Prejohn," and "Skating" are from *The Domestic Life* (University of Pittsburgh Press, 1994). "Honeymoon" and "The Prejohn" first appeared in *The Georgia Review*. "Pennies" previously appeared in *The Southern Review*. Copyright © 1994 by Hunt Hawkins. Reprinted by permission of the University of Pittsburgh Press.

Justice: "A Winter Ode to the Old Men of Lummus Park, Miami, Florida" and "Variations on a Text by Vallejo" are from *A Donald Justice Reader* (University Press of New England, 1991). Copyright © 1991 by Donald Justice. Reprinted by permission of the author.

Kershner: "Responsibilities" appeared in *The Georgia Review*. "Tantrum" appeared in *Tampa Review*. "What It Is" appeared in *The Florida Review*. "Dredging" appeared in *Poetry*. Reprinted by permission of the author.

Kirby: "I Think I Am Going to Call My Wife Paraguay," "Complicity," and "Baths" are from *Saving the Young Men of Vienna* (University of Wisconsin Press, 1987). Reprinted by permission of the author.

Knapp: "Fernando : Life : Time" was published in *Write in Our Midst*.

Kolodinsky: "march" appeared in *Whetstone*. "Inventing the Wind" appeared in *Alaska Quarterly Review*. "In Carroll County, New Hampshire" appeared in *Kalliope*. "Absence" appeared in *The Florida Review*. Reprinted by permission of the author.

Kronen: "The World Before Them" appeared in *The Paris Review*. "In the Hangar of Brisbee, Oklahoma, 1933" appeared in *The Virginia Quarterly Review*. "Mayflies" first appeared in *Boulevard* and then, along with "The Awful Balance," in *Empirical Evidence* (University of Georgia Press, 1992). Reprinted by permission of the author and University of Georgia Press.

LeForge: "Anting," "The Secret Life of Moles," "Those Moments That Make Us Remember We're Still Alive," and "Sweater" are from *The Secret Life of Moles* (Anhinga Press, 1992). Reprinted by permission of the author.

Meinke: "Scars" appeared in *The Atlantic Monthly*. "The Attack" appeared in *The Georgia Review*. "The Perch" first appeared in *Grand Street* and then in *Liquid Paper: New and Selected Poems*. "Azaleas" was first published in *Poetry* and then in *Trying to Surprise God*, and was reprinted in *Liquid Paper*. "Liquid Paper" first appeared in *The New Virginia Review* and in *The Spectator* and then in *Liquid Paper*. Copyright © 1991 by Peter Meinke. Reprinted by permission of the University of Pittsburgh Press.

Miller: "Obsession" first appeared in *Southern Poetry Review* and was reprinted in *The Contemporary Anthology Series: #3: Cross-Fertilization, The Human Spirit as Place*. "Rowing" appeared in *Tricks for Trade*. Reprinted by permission of the author.

Mitchell: "From the Journals of the Frog Prince" appeared in *The Water Inside the Water* (HarperCollins 1983). "Havana Birth" and "The Kiss" appeared in *Rapture* (HarperCollins 1993). Reprinted by permission of the author and HarperCollins.

Morton: "Florida Prelude" appeared in *Southern Poetry Review*. "River Rats" and "In a Tree Stand West of Raleigh" appeared in *Gray's Sporting Journal*. "Intimations" appeared in *Outlook*. Reprinted by permission of the author.

Nable: "A Late Night Telegram to Dr. Christiaan Barnard" appeared in *Red Bass #7*. "The Elephant Mother and Her Baby at the Tampa Carnival" appeared in *SunDog*. "The Fish Man" appeared in *Apalachee Quarterly*. Reprinted by permission of the author.

Rousseau: "J. Ford in the Water Hyacinths" appeared in *South Coast Poetry Journal*. "They Write from Great Distances" appeared in a special Alaska, Yukon and Points Northwest issue of *McCann's Poetry Society Journal*. Reprinted by permission of the author.

Sanford: "Hurricane! Alex!" first appeared in *Black Ice* and then in *Only the Nude Can Redeem the Landscape* (Apalachee Press). "Traveling Through Ports that Begin with 'M'" first appeared in *Mississippi Mud*, and then in *American Poetry Since 1970: Up Late*, and in *Only the Nude Can Redeem the Landscape*, and, in French translation, in *Aires*. Reprinted by permission of the author and Apalachee Press.

Sapia: "The Fertile Crescent" originally appeared in *Poem* and then in *The Fertile Crescent* (Anhinga Press, 1983). Reprinted by permission of the author.

Acknowledgments

Schmitt: "Under Desks" appeared in *The Nation*. "A Day at the Beach" appeared in *Massachusetts Review*. "Homecoming," "Glance" and "Tin Ear" appeared in *Country Airport* (Copper Beech Press, 1989). Reprinted by permission of the author and Copper Beech Press.

Shepherd: "First Questions" appeared in *The G.W. Review*. "Girls at Confirmation" appeared in *The Iowa Review*. Reprinted by permission of the author.

Shomer: "Sun and Moon in Mrs. Sussman's Tap Dancing Class" appeared in *Stalking the Florida Panther* (Washington, DC, The Word Works, 1987). "Cadillac" appeared in *The New Criterion*. "Elegy and Rant for My Father" appeared in *Poetry*. "Floating Islands" appeared in *The Atlantic Monthly*. "Global Aphasia" first appeared in *The Madison Review* and then in *This Close to the Earth* (University of Arkansas Press, 1992). Reprinted by permission of the author.

Skellings: "The Leningrad Writers Conference 1942" and "Incantations" first appeared in *Heart Attacks* (University of Florida Presses, 1976). "Heartwood" appeared in *Face Value* (University of Florida Presses, 1977). Reprinted by permission of the author.

Weightman: "My Children Know Reggae" previously appeared in *Q Magazine*. "A Prayer for My Quadroon Daughter" appeared in *The Devil's Millhopper*. "On Monroe Street" appeared in *New York Quarterly*. Reprinted by permission of the author.

Note: A sincere effort has been made to obtain permission to reproduce copyrighted material in *Isle of Flowers*. Please notify Anhinga Press of any inadvertent omissions, and we will include formal acknowledgment in subsequent editions of this work. Also, we have made every effort to contact all winners of the Florida Individual Artist Fellowship for Poetry. Anhinga Press sincerely apologizes to anyone we may have missed.